P9-CSU-661

RETURN TO DIGNITY

'I went through so many emotions as I read Return to Dignity... sorrow, anger, sadness and ultimately joy. I couldn't put this book down. The stories of these women who overcame seemingly insurmountable odds will capture your heart, and inspire you. This is a book that needed to be written. This is a book that not only tells hard-to-believe stories of capture and abuse, but also tells of rescue, hope and restoration. You won't be the same after you read it.'

HOLLY WAGNER, PASTOR,
OASIS CHURCH, LOS ANGELES, CALIFORNIA

'It has been one of the greatest honours of our lives to have met some of the beautiful and heroic women that Marilyn writes about in her book, Return to Dignity. We have personally witnessed the miracles firsthand that are the magnificent fruit of the work of Living Hope. These are stories of lives that must be told. They are stories of hope, redemption, victory and a return to true dignity. In a world where darkness often seems to triumph, these stories remind us of the goodness and faithfulness of our God even in the most desperate situations and places on earth.'

JOHN AND HELEN BURNS, PASTORS,
RELATE CHURCH, VANCOUVER, CANADA

'I will never forget my first trip to visit Marilyn in Uganda. It changed my world forever. My capacity was challenged, my comfort disturbed and my heart ruined for more of Jesus.

This book, which has come at such a great price, will take every reader on a similar heart-felt journey. It is like reading of heaven's love story for earth. Its pages show how the divine is drawn to the most broken, how His love lights the darkest places, and how with tenacious faith and powerful prayers we can change our world. Thank you, beautiful Marilyn, for taking us on this life changing journey with you. I pray that as a result, many more will find a return to dignity.'

CHARLOTTE GAMBILL, SENIOR ASSOCIATE PASTOR,
THE ABUNDANT LIFE CHURCH, BRADFORD, ENGLAND

'I have often wished everyone could meet Marilyn Skinner, because to meet her is to be at once challenged and changed! Return to Dignity is your introduction. These pages are a testament of how God will take our obedience and relentless love and faith to weave a tapestry of His redemption. Living Hope is reshaping a torn nation by turning its broken, brutalized daughters into ambassadors of heaven.'

LISA BEVERE, AUTHOR AND SPEAKER,
MESSENGER INTERNATIONAL

RETURN TO
DIGNITY
STORIES OF HOPE, FAITH, COURAGE AND TRANSFORMATION
MARILYN SKINNER

WITH

STEPHANIE MOTZ

&

JAMES SKINNER

FOREWORD BY BOBBIE HOUSTON

Published by Watoto
©2012 Watoto. All rights reserved.
Printed in China

No part of this publication may be reproduced in any form or by any means without prior written permission from the publisher.

Scripture quotations, unless otherwise indicated, are taken from THE MESSAGE. Copyright © by Eugene H. Peterson, 1993, 1994, 1995. Used by permission of NavPress Publishing Group.

Scripture quotations marked (NIV) are taken from the Holy Bible, New International Version ®, NIV®. Copyright © 1973, 1978, 1994, 2011 by Biblica, Inc. ™ Used by permission of Zondervan. All rights reserved worldwide. www.zondervan.com.

Design and photography by Stephanie Motz and James Skinner from Fakeleft, except:
author's photograph by James Ssekajja;
photography and design on pages 195-196 by Watoto.

All photographs are copyright of Fakeleft except: pages, 30, 54, 66, 74, 84, 112, 113, 118, 166, 184 -187, 190, 191 and author's photograph, which are copyright of Watoto.

All photographs remain the exclusive property of the copyright owners and may not be used without permission.

Cover design by Sheri Meyer and James Skinner.

ISBN 978-0-9852064-0-6

TABLE OF CONTENTS

Foreword   9

Introduction   11

1. Prossy Acayo: Guns and Grace   23

2. Rosemary Birungi: After the Flood   45

3. Mary Fiona Akello: Heart of a Servant, Hands of a Nurse   69

4. Florence Nanfuka: Beauty Beyond Any Price   87

5. Lucy Laker: Escape Into Hope   105

6. Robinah Nakkonde: A Light in the Dark   123

7. Jennifer Amony: Finding Forgiveness   141

8. Viola Lutara: It Took a Village   159

Afterword   175

ACKNOWLEDGEMENTS

I want to express special thanks to the women who have allowed me to share their stories. I admire your courage and strength. Your stories have changed my life and I am grateful to each one of you.

To everybody who made this book possible - translators, team leaders, and the media team at Watoto Church. Your dedication and commitment to Jesus and His cause inspire me.

My in-laws, Robert and Doris Skinner, invested their lives in the people of Africa for more than 50 years. Still, as passionate as ever, they graciously edited this book.

The Living Hope team in Uganda work selflessly, and have made countless personal sacrifices to bring hope where it is needed most. You are simply the best.

Gary, my one and only true love, thanks for believing in me. You make me so much better and I simply adore you.

To my grandmother,
Rosetta Mable Dawson,
who taught me
the true meaning of dignity.

"I know their pain and will make them as good as new.
They'll get a fresh start, as if nothing had ever happened.
And why? Because I am their very own God,
I'll do what needs to be done for them...I've set them free -
Oh, how they'll flourish!"

- Zechariah 10:6

BOBBIE HOUSTON
FOREWORD

The value, dignity and freedom of all humankind is of paramount concern to God. He is deeply aware of the complexities we face, the challenges we encounter and the evil that too often assails the innocent and undeserving. He has a strategized plan for the welfare of earth's sons and daughters and gave the ultimate sacrifice of His beloved Son in order to set humanity right again.

This compelling collection of heart-wrenching and yet inspiring stories, is because God's redemptive heart beats within that of Gary and Marilyn Skinner, and those with whom they share this ministry.

Their devotion, commitment and courage in the face of astounding challenge and opposition reflects all that is Christ-like in this fight for what the Bible describes as "our future and hope."

These are stories of value stolen and value miraculously restored. My prayer is that Return to Dignity will move you in a miraculous way also and that together we will continue to be men and women with a commitment to watch over and be one another's keepers. My prayer is that not only will these women be recipients of His saving grace, but that multitudes of others will be restored also because they had the courage to share their darkest hours.

On a personal note, I am humbled and grateful that God allowed our lives to collide with this Ugandan miracle. In doing so, the strength of our collective lives and the ripple effect of an awakened Church, has enabled a holy and heaven-inspired alliance of response and solution.

The battles are not over, all are not rescued and the war against value continues, but as we align our hearts with His, the victories in Uganda, Africa and beyond will be ours. Thank you Marilyn, and thank you Living Hope sisters for the inspiration you bring to us.

Bobbie Houston,

Senior Pastor
Hillsong Church, Australia

MARILYN SKINNER
INTRODUCTION

Every little girl has a dream; a dream of one day growing up, of having a career, of finding a husband that will treat her with love and respect. She dreams of forming her own family, of having her own home and finding security. But many women in Africa never get that chance. Their dreams are stolen from them at a very young age, and their future is decided for them by people in their lives who do not value them. Many girls often don't get a chance to go to school, let alone finish their education. As they grow, they become dependent on the men in their lives. They usually don't own property and have no access to financial resources. Many of them are never given the opportunity to develop, to excel and to become leaders. Poverty, war, disease, and abandonment rob millions of African women of hope and dignity.

I've lived in Africa since 1979 and when I first arrived in Uganda in 1983 I was overwhelmed by the devastation I encountered. My husband and I came to Kampala to plant Watoto Church, an English-speaking congregation in the heart of Uganda's capital.

Kampala was a city in ruins. The streets were empty and the businesses that lined them were scarred by bullets, bombs and decades of neglect. The land was fertile and abundant, yet, many people were hungry. Often I wanted to escape the chaos and return to Canada, especially when our lives were in danger. Several times our home was raided and our family was held at gunpoint and robbed. The city was filled with violence, rape and death. We heard gunfire every night and in the morning our friends and colleagues would address us with the perfectly Ugandan greeting "Well survived."

But, God showed Himself strong, and through every trial He reinforced our faith and commitment to the plan He had for us. I thought my life was tough, and for a girl who was born and raised in Bowmanville, Canada, it certainly wasn't easy. Absolutely nothing could have prepared me for life in Uganda. But, the more I learned of the daily struggles my African sisters endured, the more my heart broke for them, because I noticed that many of them were denied every basic opportunity.

In the late 1980's and early 90's, Uganda was the epicentre of Africa's AIDS crisis. At the time HIV was mysterious to many, and scientists had not yet developed the antiretroviral medications (ARVs) that so effectively prolong the life of AIDS patients today. In those early days, if you caught the virus, death was a certainty. I, like every Ugandan I know, lost people I dearly loved. My heart broke when I held my friend Diana Mubiru in my arms and watched her waste away. She was once beautiful, and vibrant; a kind and loving role-model to the youth in our church. But now her body was a frail skeleton and her skin and flesh were rotting as she died from AIDS. When I reached over and hugged her, she burst into tears and shied away in shame because she felt so devalued. She was 26 when she died and I loved and grieved for her, like a sister.

In 1993, Gary and I started Watoto Child Care Ministries to rescue orphans. Watoto has placed thousands of children into new homes and has given them a new family that is headed by a loving mother. When their parents died, they were robbed of hope and opportunity, but now they are growing up in an environment of love. Through Watoto, these children are raised to be the next generation of African leaders

I believe that Africa's greatest resource is her women waiting to be empowered. Women are key in fighting poverty and in community development. So in 2008, Watoto Church started Living Hope to rescue vulnerable women. Through Living Hope we help keep mothers alive, and we restore them to dignity, so that they can raise their own children.

I learned from the experiences of another friend, Viola Lutara, that a community of loving and caring people can intervene to save the lives of those who can not possibly manage by themselves. Viola's husband James, died as a result of AIDS before ARVs became available, but it wasn't long before the medicines were developed and they started making their way into the country. I saw how Viola's friends, family and church members gathered around her and kept her alive. They made personal and costly sacrifices. They gave their time, their money and whatever else was necessary to ensure that she could buy her medicine. Every month, in a consistent effort to save her life, they scraped together $1,500; and Viola survived.

Today, Viola is the director of Living Hope and she oversees the operations of a community of people from all around the world that is restoring hope and dignity to the lives of thousands of women.

If it had not been for the people who intentionally invested themselves in her survival, Viola would not be alive today. The power of her story is that people did care and Viola did live, and today, by living a life of excellence and influence Viola improves the world. It's impossible to say how many women are out there at this very moment who have given up all hope and are ready to die. But, I've learned that like-minded, caring individuals, with a heart for justice, can save lives and make an extraordinary difference in our world. Living Hope is a story of empowerment that lifts women from a kingdom of desperation to a kingdom of purpose, as they take their place in society as pillars in their communities.

These women were victims of circumstances that they didn't create. Some of them were sold into marriage as children. Others were infected with HIV by unfaithful husbands who had many wives and mistresses, before being abandoned and stigmatised by their communities. Some little girls were abducted by rebels of the Lord's Resistance Army (LRA) and forced to become soldiers and sex slaves. All of them were exploited and suffered horrors that made them feel worthless and incapable.

No one did more to help hurting, vulnerable women than Jesus. He changed the status of women more than anyone on the planet. Jesus modelled a gospel that translates love into justice, and true justice is putting wrong things right. At Living Hope we introduce these women to the power of His redeeming love. We walk a difficult journey with them, revisiting their pasts to help them find healing and forgiveness. Our team of psychologists combine the best international practices with those of highly skilled local trauma counsellors, to provide appropriate and relevant care as the women learn to deal with their hardships. As they heal and begin to understand that they are loved, that they are capable of doing great things, the women start to believe in themselves again. They learn that their stories aren't over and, though they can't rewrite the past, they can regain control of their future.

We disciple them. We ensure they have access to ARVs and other necessary health care. We give them food rations to make sure they stay strong and healthy. We equip them with skills through vocational training. They learn to be tailors, to make paper beads and jewellery, to produce peanut butter and to harvest honey. We employ them at our workshop where they earn a salary, and when they graduate from the program we give them a small loan for them to invest in their own businesses.

At Living Hope, we know that change is possible because we've witnessed amazing transformations in the lives of so many women. They are examples of God's beautiful plan to reconcile us to Himself, and they have so much to teach us. God is returning these women to dignity through people like the dedicated staff at the Living Hope centres in Uganda, as well as our partners and sponsors all around the world who have come alongside their African sisters in their journey toward healing and restoration.

Return to Dignity is the story of women who realise that they don't have to be victims. Instead, they understand that they have the potential to rise above their circumstances. They can be empowered. They can shine as beacons of hope in their communities.

God has a purpose for every one of us. We all have our own struggles and I pray that the stories in this book will inspire you through whatever trials you face in life. I pray that you will find strength, courage and hope. God can renew our broken lives and make something beautiful out of our ashes. I believe that when He sees us when we are in pain, when we are lonely or lost, He wants to gather us up in His arms and whisper His love into us, to transform us. He wants to return us all to dignity . We were created in His image - and He uses ordinary people, you and me, to introduce the change that our hurting world so desperately needs.

Kampala city skyline.

"Living Hope is a place where vulnerable women come to be redeemed, adored, cared for and given back their life."

- MARILYN SKINNER

PROSSY ACAYO
GUNS AND GRACE

"...You'll get a brand new name straight from the mouth of God.
You'll be a stunning crown in the palm of God's hand... No more will
anyone call you rejected...You'll be called My Delight." - Isaiah 62:2

Prossy dodged the bullets that were coming from in front of her, and as they flew by, she could hear them scream and rip through the leaves and branches of the bushes where she was hiding. Her brigade of 12 soldiers was under attack from government troops. At just 14 she was an accomplished, battle-hardened fighter in the Lord's Resistance Army and one of the oldest in the field that day. The Ugandan army wanted her dead.

Together with 11 other children she was on a mission to steal food from a nearby village, when they fell into a government ambush. A grenade exploded in the middle of their group and she knew instantly that many of her comrades were dead. The impact threw Prossy to the ground. She collapsed next to one of the older boys and felt his blood splatter across her face. She believed she was going to die. Prossy had often thought of dying on the battlefield and sometimes wished for it. Her life, which at one time held so much promise, was now defined by the pain she was forced to inflict on others, and she was tired of fighting.

She had seen friends die and watched as they were tortured in front of her. Others had fallen on the battlefield and she had walked away from their corpses, leaving them to rot where they lay. And not all of the wounded, whom she had rescued and carried back to safety, survived. Sometimes it seemed that life was more painful than death and so she did not fear death. But at this moment, with her life in such danger, Prossy felt a strange resilience, a silent strength that overwhelmed her and gave her the will to live. Prossy wasn't looking for revenge, she just wanted to go home.

Abduction

She thought of her mother and baby brother Kenneth, who was only two on the night when the rebels broke down the door of her hut and grabbed Prossy from her mother's grasp. It was in December, 1994, when Prossy was taken. She returned home after school with her brothers, Dennis and Geoffrey. Geoffrey, who was sixteen at the time, helped the younger ones with their homework and then Prossy and Dennis joined the children in the neighbourhood to play. Prossy loved her brothers and looked up to them. And she was so proud to be baby Kenneth's big sister. That evening, the LRA were in the area and Prossy's mother wrapped Kenneth on her back and prepared the children to go to hide in the grass. But, the sky turned somber, the wind howled and lightning pierced through the dark clouds, briefly illuminating the sky. Prossy's mother decided that they would sleep at home that night because of the oncoming storm.

Their homestead sat on top of a gentle hill, surrounded by hundreds of mango trees that had been planted by Prossy's great grandfather. In the season when the trees were full of mangoes and they were ripe and falling, Prossy's family would welcome strangers and travellers passing through. They would climb the trees to pick the fruit and they would fill their sacks and take them to the market.

That night Prossy slept in a hut with her aunt and cousins. At around 2:00 a.m. the dog suddenly began to bark and everyone woke up. A few seconds later they heard the sound of rebel soldiers kicking in the door. Geoffrey was quick to realise what was happening and he managed to escape, but the rebels captured Prossy and Dennis.

They put Prossy in a line of a dozen other boys and girls and tied them together, like slaves, with a rope fastened tight around their waists. In the confused panic of her abduction, Prossy heard two gunshots and, as she turned, she saw Dennis lying with blood pouring from wounds in his chest. But before she could react she felt the chord tear into the skin around her hips and she was dragged away into the darkness. With each step that stole her away from home she heard the screams of her brother as he cried out in agony. The sounds of him dying slowly faded into a black silence. By the time the neighbours arrived in the morning Dennis was dead. He was 12 years old. But for Prossy, still only 10, her new life of horrors was only beginning.

The abducted children were then forced to walk for several hours before the group sat down to rest. In the morning, all of the children were released, except for Prossy. She was forced to walk for many days alongside a group of men, and eventually they arrived at a place called Palabek, which was the rebel's main camp in Northern Uganda. Two weeks later another group of abducted children arrived. Amongst them was one of Prossy's neighbours. This is how she came to learn of her brother Dennis' death.

Now, in this forsaken wilderness, strewn with bullets and blood, Prossy determined to live. Kenneth would be six now, walking and talking, and getting into untold mischief. Prossy ached to see him again. She gathered her strength and courage and focused her thoughts. She checked herself for injuries and felt a throbbing pain in her arm. A piece of shrapnel was embedded near the joint of her elbow. Her flesh was torn and blood poured out of the wound, but she knew that if she escaped capture that she could survive. She stood up and surveyed the carnage. Seven of her brigade were dead and the other four were badly injured. She spotted Ojara who was the youngest in her group. He was alive but had been shot in the leg and couldn't walk. She thought of the horrors the injured survivors would face when captured. It was said that when government troops captured child soldiers they beat and tortured them before finishing them off with a bullet in the head. There was no time. She had to make a quick decision.

She grabbed Ojara and slung him onto her back and began to carry him. She hoped to find the path that lead to their camp, but she soon realised that she was lost. She heard the sound of the soldiers following close behind but she pressed relentlessly on, forcing her way through thick stalks of grass and thorny-branched thicket. Eventually she came to a small river and waded into the water. Ojara's body hung limply over her back. Even though he was a small boy, she could not carry him indefinitely and her strength was beginning to diminish. She waded downstream for some distance before coming to a small clearing on the opposite bank. She finally felt that they were safe and so she settled with

Ojara under a tree to rest.

Prossy had been in the bush for four years and her childhood had long since been stolen from her. The things that she was forced to do had stripped her of dignity. She had been taught to steal, to destroy crops and to burn down homes. She had learned how to terrorise a community and she now understood how to kill. Picking mangoes and playing amongst the trees of her grandfather's orchard, tickling her baby brother and feeding off of his irresistible laughter - these were distant memories, dreams she hid in a secret, unmolested corner of her heart, a sacred place not yet tarnished by the everyday evil of her life. It was in these moments, when fighting for her life, that she recalled those happy thoughts, and they gave her courage to carry on.

She was one of the boys and girls, more than 30,000 of them, who had been stolen from their homes and forced to fight for the LRA against the government of Uganda. The rebels believed that if trained well, children made the best soldiers. They had seen how, once removed from their families and robbed of every imaginable prospect or hopeful ambition, these children had nothing to live for and were fearless in combat. And so to make their separation permanent, the rebels would often force the children to return to their villages to abduct other children, or to kill their own families. Children who refused to carry out these orders were made examples of and were often killed in the most horrific manner. Stories were told of children being beaten to death with sticks and clubs or being bitten to death by other children who were forced to prey on their victims like wild animals. Their abductors supervised these horrors with trigger-happy fingers at the ready.

And so Prossy had killed in the hope that she would live. In time she came to be known as a reliable and trustworthy soldier. She never left her ammunition behind during a skirmish and she cared for her comrades. In the two years since, as a girl of 12, she had first fired a gun in battle, she had risen to the rank of corporal. But her commanders' efforts to permanently detach her from her family had failed. The source of her courage lay only in the hope that one day she would escape from her captors. She kept that hope alive with the simple idea that one day she would return to the embrace of her mother and father.

But, to discourage any thoughts of escape, the rebel commanders told the children that if they returned home, their communities would kill them and besides, nobody wanted them because they were now murderers. Even if they tried to escape, they would never see their families again. The only way to return home was to fight and to win. Still, some children tried to escape and when they were captured they were publicly tortured and executed to discourage those who held similar ambitions. Yet, even though she had seen and heard all of these things, Prossy never gave up hope. When she faced death or was being raped by her lieutenant "husband," Prossy contemplated the risk and determined to flee the bush.

As she sat under the tree, nursing Ojara's wound, Prossy thought she recognised an opportunity to escape, but fear crept into her heart and she abandoned the idea. If they didn't die in battle that day, she was convinced they would die under that tree. She gathered her bag and emptied its contents onto the ground. She was looking for some dry beans and maize but there was nothing to eat. She found some plastic bags among Ojara's things and so she collected some water from the river and boiled it over a small flame she had made. Experience had taught her which wild plants were edible and she found some roots and a type of wild spinach which she put into the bags of boiling water until they were cooked. They ate together, and then she gathered some dry wild grass and made a bed and watched over Ojara as he slept.

Hiding in the Grass

Prossy had been sleeping outside, hiding in the darkness of night since she was a little girl. When the war began and the LRA started abducting children, many people would spend the night away from their homes on nights they suspected the rebels were close. And as darkness fell each night thousands of children would walk miles from their rural communities to hide in town centres, schools and hospitals where they hoped that the government would protect them. Many of them would sleep on the covered sidewalks or the porches of the traders' shops. In the morning they would get up and walk back home. They were known as the "night commuters."

Prossy lived far from the town, in a tiny village in northern Uganda. When her family had to hide they would sleep outside somewhere not too far from her house, under the tall grass. Her father was a government soldier and in order to protect the identity of his family he moved to the nearby town of Kitgum. During school holidays, Prossy's family would visit her father in the town and her mother would often work there as a nurse. Prossy observed her mother tending the sick and nursing wounds. She dreamed of one day following in her mother's footsteps.

Typical rural scene near Gulu, in northern Uganda.

"The source of her courage lay only in the hope that one day she would escape from her captors."

When Prossy stayed at the village, every day at dusk, when the sun set over the mango trees, her mother and her widowed aunt, who lived in the neighbouring compound, gathered their children and walked together to find a place near a stream or river to hide during the night. There they would create a small tent, called a bung, out of sticks and grass. Each bung was big enough to fit three people. Prossy slept beside her two elder brothers, Geoffrey and Dennis while her mother slept in another tent with their youngest brother, Kenneth.

Prossy grew accustomed to observing the behaviour of birds and animals and learned how to understand their warnings. During the day, the agoga bird warned them of danger by flying around their compound unsettled, before hiding inside the hole of a tree and sounding out its song of caution. At night Prossy and her brothers would lie in their open bung, watching the night sky, listening for the ominous sound of the owl. In her culture, the call of the owl is a sign of danger and so she learned to fear it. Sometimes they would be woken by insects, and scratching at their painful bites, they would discover a nest of safari ants attacking their bung. Many times they had to move and rebuild their shelter because animals had destroyed it. They were often startled by the faintest sounds, and even when they suspected it was just a frog or a mouse, they would get up and quietly scout the area.

Spending the night outside, under the stars, hungry and far from home, falling asleep to the sound of bullets, was familiar to her. Yet, she still missed the feeling of sleeping in her bed, away from the biting insects and falling rain. And even though nights in the bush became a regular pattern of her life she never grew accustomed to the fear that penetrated her heart when darkness fell and imagined dangers became unseen realities. She knew that out there in the blackness that surrounded her, there were people who wanted to abduct her.

In the morning, when she went to school, the headmaster would read to the assembled students the names of the children who had been taken during the night. One day he read the name of her friend Agnes. She hoped that Agnes would escape and return home, but she never saw her friend again. When children did manage to escape captivity, they would share the horrors they had experienced. One boy returned and told Prossy that when the rebels abducted children as young as Prossy they forced them to slaughter another person so that they could never return home. "If you try to escape," he said, "they will slaughter you in the same way." Prossy was terrified.

Violence and Violation

The camp at Palabek was like a large village and more than a thousand people lived there. Prossy was immediately assigned to a house where she had to collect water, cook and clean for a rebel commander called Okello. She learned that these would be her duties until she reached the age when she could be displayed before a group of commanders and selected as a wife by one of them. Or, if Okello wanted, he could keep her for himself. Once she was selected as a wife she would then accompany her "husband" in battle and carry his ammunition, food and water to the frontline. Pregnant women and mothers stayed back at camp and cared for their children.

Prossy had been in captivity for only a month when Okello was called to battle and Prossy was left under the care of a 50 year-old lieutenant called Acam Kwe. It was decided at the same time that Prossy's group would move to another camp in South Sudan. The commanders realised that this provided an opportunity for the children to escape, so at night they would surround the youngsters and sleep in groups encircling them.

One night, Acam Kwe called for Prossy and she was terrified. She was only ten years old, so she followed his orders and walked with him until they arrived at a place where he had prepared a bed of grass and blankets. She understood his intentions. They were not far from the group, so Acam Kwe brought his hand to her throat and began to force his grip on her neck. He told her to stay silent or he would kill her. And then he raped her. When he was finished, he raped her again. He did not stop until the morning and then he got up and before walking away he warned her that if she spoke of this to anyone she would die. Prossy remained there bruised and bleeding and she could not walk. Her legs were weak, and her body, where Acam Kwe had abused her was wounded.

And deep inside her, in a place that was not physical, a place that could not be touched or caressed, she was torn and changed forever. A seed was planted, and as it grew it became a memory of violence and violation. She had become to herself, nothing. And so she embraced bitterness and hatred. To survive, she thought, she must fight for herself. Finally she was able to return to the group, but she kept bleeding. She was afraid and she said nothing, but when Okello, returned from battle he noticed that Prossy was in constant pain and that she kept wiping blood from between her legs.

Her wounds were not healing and she was afraid they would become infected, but she was also afraid to reveal the secret that was destroying her. Okello continued to press the issue, and eventually Prossy couldn't contain it any longer and the truth burst out of her. She was carried to a hospital in Sudan where she spent seven months recovering. There, nurses applied compresses on her legs and wounded body. They washed her with water and salt to fight off infection and they massaged her limbs.

When she recovered she had to return to camp where, to her horror, she discovered that Acam Kwe had requested that Okello allow her to become a baby-sitter to his children. Okello may have had a few concerns, but because Prossy had been raped by Acam Kwe he did not want her for himself and so he agreed to the proposal. Prossy was not given any choice, instead she was forced to move in with her abuser and to serve and submit to him. She washed his clothes; she cooked his food; she nursed his wounds when he returned wounded from battle; she cared for his children.

He raped her when he grew tired of his wives.

Soon Acam Kwe's wives began to notice the way that Prossy's condition was deteriorating. They pleaded for her and one night, when he demanded that she be brought to him, one of them approached him and begged that Prossy be left alone. She was only 12 and was not ready to become a wife. Acam Kwe swatted aside the woman and stormed over to the hut where Prossy was staying. There he grabbed a hold of her and dragged her to his hut. He raped her all night long.

In the morning he haughtily threw her into the arms of his wives as if she was a soiled rag. The women were furious at the abuse Prossy had endured. She was emotionally broken and physically destroyed. She was nothing. Together they went to complain to the commanders in charge of their unit, but Acam Kwe was already there giving his own account of what had happened. He told the commanders that he wanted Prossy to be his wife but that she was unwilling to fulfill her sexual obligations to him and that she had disrespected him. Her fate was quickly determined. The commanders decided to use Prossy as an example for all the other young girls – "this is what happens to a girl who refuses to be a wife," they said – and they called the whole camp together to witness her punishment.

From the assembled crowd five boys were called forward and they were told to each collect 200 sticks. When they returned they were made to lie down on the ground and, surrounded by hundreds of witnesses, each one of them was beaten with a stick until it broke. Then they commanded the boys to get up, to take the remaining sticks and to beat Prossy in the same way until every stick had broken. Prossy was lashed ruthlessly. Her clothes ripped and shred into tatters. Her skin welted and then ripped open. She felt the pressure of her blood pulsating and pounding in her brain. Sweat and tears began to mix with the blood that was trickling into her eyes and mouth. She could taste the elements of her own body and she clutched at the dirt beneath her as she cried for mercy. But in this place there was no mercy, only submission, a humiliation purchased through vengeance and blood. Her body, still bruised from a night of violent rape, could not endure any more torture and she lost consciousness.

Her commanders believed that they had taught her a valuable

lesson and that her experience would make her callous - tough enough to become a soldier. When they thought she was finally ready, they instructed her to steal the gun and uniform from an injured Ugandan soldier. When, at the age of twelve, she had done this, they taught her how to assemble and use her new weapon. Soon she could fire her gun and as her aim improved, she was sent into battle where she had to carry Acam Kwe's food and ammunition. It was not long before she had to defend herself and she killed her first enemy soldier. Her initiation was complete when she was sent to abduct other children and force them into captivity. Now, she was both victim and perpetrator.

Return

Prossy spent one week in the wilderness nursing Ojara back to health. They were running low on supplies and every day, she thought it would be her last. Still, she managed to keep Ojara alive and they survived alone in the bush until they were discovered by an LRA foot patrol. The rebels found Prossy and Ojara semi-conscious and so they carried them back to their camp. Ojara survived, but he was transferred to a different brigade and Prossy never saw him again.

She now put aside all thoughts of escape and she resigned herself to the idea that she would be a rebel soldier, an outlaw, until the day Acam Kwe died. She had to wait another five years before he was killed in battle. She didn't mourn his death, but she feared that another commander would claim her as his own. Soon after Acam Kwe's death a new group of abducted children arrived at camp and she recognised some of them from her village.

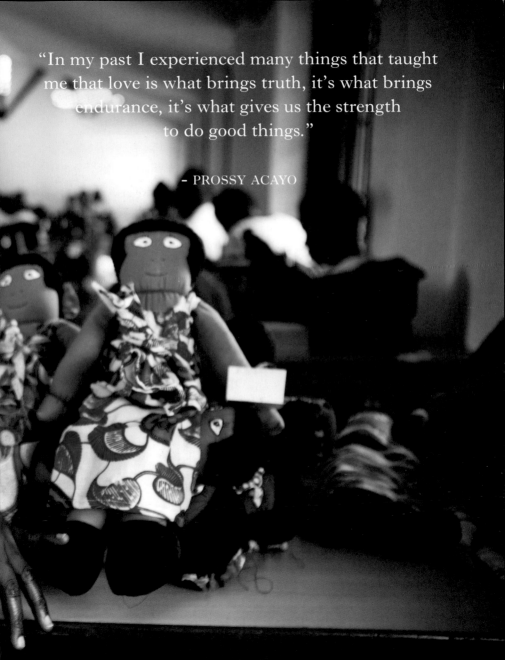

"In my past I experienced many things that taught me that love is what brings truth, it's what brings endurance, it's what gives us the strength to do good things."

- PROSSY ACAYO

One of them told her that her parents were dead. She thought of Kenneth and wondered who was taking care of him.

She thought of the many times she was told to fight if she ever wanted to see her parents again. She thought of the night she was abducted and how she never had a chance to say goodbye or to hug them one more time. She felt cheated, defeated and angry. A few weeks later she learned that she was pregnant and as she thought about the prospect of raising a little boy or girl in these circumstances she decided to run away. Prossy was 18 years old when she escaped after living in captivity for almost nine years. She fled until she was rescued by the Sudanese army and taken into protective custody by the United Nations.

Eventually she was repatriated to Gulu, the largest town in Northern Uganda, but she had nowhere to go and no means of survival. At the time World Vision was working to reunite "returnees" with their family and to integrate them back into their community. They succeeded in finding one of Prossy's aunts who agreed to take her in. But when the aunt discovered that Prossy was pregnant she chased her away. Prossy felt lonely, abandoned and rejected by her family. She even began to wonder if she had made a mistake by escaping from the LRA. But then one small act of kindness changed everything.

A lady, who worked at the World Vision centre in Gulu recognised her desperate situation and took Prossy home to live with her. She started taking tailoring classes and she stayed in that home and gave birth on the floor. Soon after the birth of her son, Prossy's brother Kenneth found her. After his parents had died Kenneth went to live with his grandmother. He was unable to finish his education but he had found a job at a hotel and this is how he was sustaining himself. He didn't make much money but he was happy to be reunited with his sister and he took Prossy home to live with him. There, with the love and comfort of her brother, Prossy began her return to dignity. A decade earlier she had been stolen from her home as an innocent girl with a promising future; now she had returned a broken and wounded woman, weighed down by the gravity of her circumstances. She had no education and the skills she had acquired during the war only served to isolate her as a murderer and a thief. She was free to go where she wanted, as she pleased, yet she found herself trapped by her traumas and she could not escape the memories of her past.

When Prossy first arrived at the Living Hope Centre she felt angry, ashamed and isolated but she was desperate. She was a single mother who had returned from the bush and felt as if she was a burden to the people in her life. She had heard an announcement on the radio calling for vulnerable women - single mothers, returnees from the bush, those who had HIV - to register at Watoto Church in Gulu, where Living Hope was offering their assistance. Though she was skeptical and wondered if she could really trust the people at Living Hope, Prossy decided she would give it a try.

Ten thousand other women showed up along with Prossy, and the staff at Living Hope realised that the need was far greater then they had imagined. Living Hope was prepared to provide immediate assistance to 1,000 women, and it was nearly impossible to choose from the massive crowd that clamoured for attention. Prossy was one of the group who were found to be the most vulnerable and she was accepted into the program's first intake.

As she walked into the hall on the first day of discipleship class she felt nervous and insecure. There were people speaking English, and she couldn't understand anything that they were saying. But then she met Gladys, Dorothy and Rosemary - Living Hope staff members who were from her community. They spoke to her in Acholi and greeted her with a loving embrace. And then she began to learn again. She began to learn that she was valuable because God loved her, and had a purpose for her life. These were revolutionary, and initially incompatible thoughts to her. Where was God in those years of torment? Where was her value when her experiences had taught her that her flesh was for the whimsical amusement of evil men? And now, after all of the traumas in her life had reduced her to emptiness, how could she find meaning and purpose in the scattered pieces of her broken life? She began to discover that in reassembling those countless fragments, and by establishing them in truth and love with a simple understanding of God's grace, she started to find direction.

One day, someone illustrated to her the meaning of value by reaching into her wallet and pulling out two identical 10,000 shilling notes. Prossy intrinsically knew their value. If she went to market with either one of the bills she could feed her family for several days. Yet, as she looked at the two notes in the lady's hand it became obvious to Prossy that in their appearance the notes were different. One was brand new. It looked as if it had never been folded or used to make a purchase. It was as if it had been released into circulation for the first time that very morning. The second note was old, creased and wrinkled. Dirt and grime had been smeared all over it and it was filthy. It looked like it had been dropped in the mud, or shoved down the inside of somebody's sweaty sock. The lady asked Prossy which of the two notes she thought could purchase more. Prossy, knowing the value of money understood that both, though different in appearance, were essentially the same.

She began to understand that her value lay not in the sum total of her life's experiences, but in what was imprinted upon her from the moment that her life began. And when Prossy understood that she was created in the image of God and that His design and desires were imprinted on her, Prossy perspective began to change. She began to understand that despite her circumstances she was actually more valuable than she could ever desire to be. Because of this understanding Prossy learned that she was able to forgive.

Her continued journey back to restoration has been a long, slow and painful one to walk. Gradually, the small acts of goodness that she experiences in her new life continue to reinforce her strength and her hope for the future. At Living Hope she has perfected her skills as a tailor and with the income she earns from her work she is able to support her family, and help Kenneth as he finishes his education.

Now, Prossy is a leader at the Living Hope Centre in Gulu, and a quality control supervisor of the new Living Hope ladies. With a gentle voice and a sweet smile, she guides them and helps them improve their skills in preparing all of the merchandise produced at the Living Hope tailoring department. She has become a signpost in her community, an example of excellence, humility and transformation. Throughout her life she has been called many things - abductee, soldier, single mother, vulnerable woman - but now her community has nicknamed her "doctor" because of the high regard in which they hold her. Prossy has become a woman of influence, battling on a different front line as she fights to change her community and return it to dignity.

ROSEMARY BIRUNGI
AFTER THE FLOOD

"Be strong. Take courage. Don't be intimidated. Don't give them a second thought because God, your God, is striding ahead of you. He's right there with you. He won't let you down; he won't leave you."
- Deuteronomy 31:6

Rosemary stared blankly at her sewing machine. The voice of her instructor at the Living Hope workshop in Kampala was an incoherent blur, and her thoughts raced in untraceable circles as she tried to make sense of the machine in front of her. Rosemary lifted her head and saw two-dozen women working with confidence and skill. They all knew what they were doing. Their hands delicately threading the spool into their machines, and their feet gently pumping the pedal as the wheels spun into action. Rosemary's thread, however, lay in a tangled mess on the desk in front of her. She could find neither the beginning nor the end.

It was her first day at Living Hope. She never wanted to be a tailor, and for much of her youth she was confident that she could be anything that she liked. She had excelled in school. She was an intelligent student with plenty of promise, but one mistake, something she immediately regretted, had set in motion a chain of events that determined the rest of her life. Everything that followed seemed to entangle, to entrap her, until, like the thread now laying in front of her, she could not make sense of anything.

She wiped the sweat off her forehead, scratched her head and stared at the exit, as she considered her escape.

Full of Promise

Rosemary came from a hardworking family of farmers. Her parents had separated when she was young and so she grew up with her uncle and her paternal grandmother in a small village near Fort Portal, in Western Uganda. She was a strong and determined girl, and though her father wasn't always present in her life, when he visited, he made sure Rosemary was doing her best in school. He wanted her to achieve great things because he believed in her.

Every day Rosemary woke up early in the morning and walked for 40 minutes until she reached the place where she collected water. As a young girl, the weight of the water was too much, and her muscles trembled as she struggled to carry it. Often, she had to stop and rest. But, as she grew older, and with practice, she learned how to lift the container, and balance it on her head without wasting a drop. She learned how to move her neck and head to counteract the movement of her body as she walked, and she could carry the water like this, balancing it on her head, for many kilometres without stopping. Only a banana leaf, that had been folded and wrapped into a cushioned ring, protected the top of her head and prevented the container from falling.

After school she worked in the garden with her grandmother. Together they made heaps of soil in neat rows and planted cuttings from the vines of potatoes that were ready to be harvested. She softened the earth with her hands and planted beans and corn. She watched over the pumpkin patch to make sure it didn't take over the garden and suffocate the other plants. Though her life wasn't easy, she grew up experiencing love and care. Her grandmother gave her many responsibilities, but, because Rosemary was the youngest child in the family, her grandmother took care to make sure nobody made Rosemary work too hard.

However, when her grandmother died, Rosemary's uncle and aunt treated her very harshly. One day, she was chopping firewood in the garden when the panqa* slipped from her hand and sliced a deep gash into her leg. Rosemary rushed back home where her aunt looked at her with suspicion and accused Rosemary of cutting herself so that she didn't have to work. Rosemary had to limp to a neighbour in order to receive treatment for her wound.

When Rosemary's mother discovered that her daughter was being mistreated, she brought Rosemary to Kampala to live with her. Rosemary's mother worked hard selling plantain bananas in the market to pay for her daughter's school fees, and Rosemary excelled. When she finished primary school she was one of the best students in her class and her mother was so proud of her. Like most Ugandan girls, Rosemary learned how to cook matooke and binyebwa*, at a young age. Rosemary helped her mother with the domestic chores, and she tended to her mother's vegetable garden. But it was at school that Rosemary showed the most promise.

*panga: local name for a machete; a long sharp knife
*matooke and binyewba: a plantain mash and peanut sauce that is the staple in much of Uganda.

Rosemary was full of confidence, and believed that if she applied herself and studied hard, she could make it to university, and eventually become a teacher. She didn't want her mother to struggle selling matooke at the market for the rest of her life. She had big dreams, and nobody who knew Rosemary doubted that she could accomplish them. But, just before her last year of high school, Rosemary became pregnant and had to drop out. She hid the pregnancy from her mother for as long as she could, but she was only prolonging the inevitable. One day, as she lay on her bed cramped up with pain, her mother became suspicious and Rosemary had to reveal her relationship with Sam, a man she had met while collecting water at the neighbour's house.

Rosemary's mother was furious. She had worked so hard; she had sacrificed every personal ambition and invested it into her daughter. She looked at Rosemary and saw so much waste. A few weeks later Rosemary had a miscarriage and had to spend two weeks in the hospital. When she returned home, she pleaded for a second chance, but her relatives and neighbours had convinced Rosemary's mother not to support Rosemary any more. A cousin came by and discussed Rosemary's future with her mother. They completely ignored Rosemary, neither acknowledging her presence nor listening to her passionate pleas. The cousin told Rosemary's mother that if Rosemary went back to school she would only become pregnant again. It would be better, he insisted, to make her go and live with the man who got her pregnant in the first place.

Lost Potential

Rosemary had lost her mother's trust and she knew that she had squandered an incredible opportunity. She had managed to stay in school for much longer than many other girls, and had performed so well. Now, Rosemary was broken and consumed by guilt. Her future was decided by a momentary indiscretion, and once her mother stopped believing in her, Rosemary's prospects disappeared. When her mother told her she had to leave the house, Rosemary had nowhere else to go so she grabbed her few belongings and moved in with Sam. They determined to make the most of their circumstances.

Rosemary lived with Sam for 10 years and together they had four children. For a while they were happy. Sam worked tirelessly to provide for his family, and they were never hungry. He was a sugar trader, buying in bulk from producers and wholesalers, and reselling it to supermarkets and other vendors. Together with his business partner, Sam travelled throughout the country collecting and packing truckloads of sugar. They would then return to the city with their payload. Sam did well from his business and he helped Rosemary to open up a small shop. She was able to secure a loan, and bought a refrigerator and a popcorn machine, and she sold snacks and beverages from her front porch. They weren't wealthy, but through hard work, Rosemary and Sam were able to send their children to school, and their businesses grew. But, as Sam's business thrived the marriage began to suffer.

Soon Rosemary began to notice that her husband spent less time at home; his business trips were getting longer; he stopped bringing food home. One day he came home, dropped off some groceries and left before Rosemary could ask him where he was going. He didn't come home that night. Rosemary became anxiously suspicious and irritated with the mystery. She confronted him when he returned, and learned of the other woman that Sam had been seeing.

Rosemary wept in anguish. An overpowering suffocation wrapped her and clung to her like a descending cloud of despair. And, like a death, it was inescapable. She loved Sam. She trusted him and had invested her hopes into the life that they were building together. Now she felt replaced and secondary. She began to think that she was a fool to have fallen for his deception. She wondered which of his words, which of his actions were true. Eventually, she arrived at a bitter loneliness. As she analysed her circumstances, Rosemary came to the conclusion that she was not loved. Maybe it was her own fault, she thought. Maybe she was too short-tempered, or, maybe her body had become unattractive. Maybe she just wasn't good enough.

She noticed that many of her friends and neighbours experienced similar heartbreak. Often they suffered in silence, even though they knew their husbands had many mistresses. Many of them feared to speak up because, if they confronted the men, they might be chased out of the house, and forced to fend for themselves on the street. But Rosemary knew that she could not accept the kind of life where she had to share a man. She made Sam choose between his family and his mistress. He chose the other woman and abandoned the family to their own fate. Rosemary continued to stay in her house, but now she had to pay the rent, and provide for the children, all by herself.

Not long after, Rosemary was robbed. While the family slept, thieves broke into their home and sprayed a gas that ensured the family didn't wake up. When Rosemary got up in the morning her fridge had been emptied, and the popcorn machine and television were gone. She tried to secure another loan, but because she was now a single mother, she was turned down. All she had were her clothes and an empty fridge. Now she had no means of income, and no way to repay the original loan she had taken to purchase the things the thieves had taken from her. Soon, she began falling behind on her payments and the bank collectors started knocking on her door. One day, they arrived with the police and Rosemary had to give them everything she owned.

Rosemary was now penniless and the landlord evicted her. One of her neighbours took pity on her and offered her a small plot of land in a swamp adjacent to his land, advising her to build a temporary structure there. Rosemary gathered scraps from people's homes - discarded pieces of wood and nails, old and rusty iron sheets, broken bricks, and cardboard boxes that were left out with the trash. She assembled all of the items into a tiny, flimsy shack, and marked out her own little piece of territory in the swamp.

Endurance

When the wind gathered the distant clouds, and the air became cold and damp, Rosemary would gather her children and prepare them for the impending flood. The rain brought gushing torrents of filth and sewage that washed down from the surrounding hills. At first, it collected in stinking pools underneath her bed, but the water level rose at an astonishing rate and soon Rosemary was up to her knees in a foul mix of mud and garbage. Even a light downpour was enough to ensure a sleepless night. At night, with the first drops of rain, Rosemary would wake her children. Together they would gather all of their possessions, pile them on their heads, and stand on the bed as they waited for the storm to pass. Sometimes they had to run through the torrential downpour and knock on their neighbours' doors, hoping that someone would give them a place to sleep through the night. When the storm was over, Rosemary had to dig her house out from under the mud.

She struggled, but somehow she managed to keep her children in school. Government subsidies, designed to enable all children to go to primary school, were not adequate to pay for school uniforms, textbooks and other school supplies. Without these items a child wouldn't be allowed to attend classes, and many children couldn't afford them. For children who wanted to go to high school, there were no government programs to help them. They had to find the money to pay for school fees before they could continue their education. Many children simply dropped out. It was a testament to Rosemary's persistence, that her children never missed school.

Rosemary joined a church, and a sense of hope began to stir up inside her as she made friends who became involved in her life. They demonstrated God's love for her through small, practical acts of kindness. They helped find a sponsor for her oldest daughter Pauline, so that she could go to high school. Pauline had excelled at primary school and, on graduating she had finished at the top of her class. Rosemary didn't want to crush her daughter's dreams. She wanted to make sure that each of her children had an equal opportunity to finish their education, but money for food and rent was scarce.

The whole family had to make sacrifices, and Rosemary was willing to humble herself to do any job that would allow her children to fulfil their ambitions. Rosemary was well educated, fluent in English, and had done reasonably well with her business before Sam had left her. But taking care of four growing children all by herself was proving too difficult for her to manage on her own. One day a neighbour came to visit, and noticed that Rosemary's youngest child was crying because he was hungry. Rosemary was embarrassed, but she was doing the best that she could. The visitor told Rosemary that she knew a family who was looking for a maid, and that this opportunity might help Rosemary to earn some extra money. Rosemary thought about it briefly. At first, she believed she was above the opportunity. She had managed to make a living from her business until the thieves had stolen her property. She believed that if she could secure another loan she might be able to open up her canteen again. Why, Rosemary thought, should she have to humble herself before her neighbours? Why should she clean their homes and scrub their toilets? But as she looked at her children and saw that they were suffering, she knew that this opportunity was a chance to re-establish herself. She swallowed her pride and agreed to take the job.

When she arrived at work the following day she was surprised to learn that she already knew the man who was now her boss. They had been in the same class in high school. Rosemary felt a sudden humiliation rush over her. She blushed and looked away timidly. How could she deal with this arrangement? How could she cope, day after day, with the comparisons that she had already begun to draw? When she looked at her boss she saw a successful man whose life seemed to have turned out much better than her own.

Next Page: Katanga Slum, in Kampala

She felt like a failure. Here was this man, whom she had solidly outperformed in school; now she was washing his socks and changing his children's soiled diapers. The man treated her with kindness and dignity, but still Rosemary felt insignificant.

One day, he sat Rosemary down and asked, "Rosemary, what happened?" Rosemary recognised that her life hadn't turned out the way that she had dreamed when she was still a young girl in school, but she loved her children, and she was determined to see them flourish. She took a second job, packing food in a factory, which paid her 2,000 shillings, less than a dollar, a week.

Evading the Truth

Occasionally she saw Sam when he stopped by to visit the children, and on one of his visits she noticed that he had lost a lot of weight. Someone told Rosemary that his girlfriend was sick and she suspected that Sam might have HIV, but Rosemary kept her thoughts to herself. She didn't want to consider the possibility that the man, who had broken her heart, had also infected her with the virus. She didn't want to know the truth because she feared it would destroy her. If she knew, she would give up hope for her future, she would become sick and she would quickly die. Her children would be left destitute, homeless, without hope. If she could only believe, if she could only convince herself that she was healthy, then she might live long enough to see her children finish school and go on to pursue their dreams. Knowing would only illuminate the severity, the barrenness of her situation. Knowing would only confirm, with certainty, her demise. But Sam died only one year after abandoning Rosemary, and his sister came to advise

Rosemary to take an HIV test.

Still, Rosemary found excuses to avoid the truth. She was too busy, too tired, or, she didn't have the money to catch a taxi to the clinic and it was too far for her to walk. But, if she caught a lingering cold, or noticed a slight rash on her skin she wondered if it meant that she was dying. Eventually she became sick and Rosemary knew that she had to confront her fears. She went to the hospital and asked for a blood test. She sat hunched over on a hard wooden bench and picked at the corner of her nails as she waited for the results.

Finally, the nurse returned with a large brown envelope and gave it to Rosemary. She turned it over in her hands clumsily, and fidgeted absentmindedly with one corner. For a moment Rosemary thought about death. She thought about her body decomposing in the earth amidst the banana groves of her childhood village. That is where they would take her corpse - if her father's family would accept it. Rosemary straightened her back and lifted her head and shoulders so that she was sitting upright and tall. She reached into the envelope and pulled out the paper that was inside, and as she read it she wept. Rosemary was not surprised, but she was still devastated. She gathered her things, stood up and walked home. She knew now, that her life was different, but she found a strange resilience, which willed her on. Rosemary decided that she would continue to find work, and to stay alive for her children.

When Pauline got cerebral malaria, Rosemary had to take her to the hospital for regular checkups. While she was waiting for the doctor to see Pauline, Rosemary noticed a long line of people waiting to receive their ARVs. Some of them looked healthy, but

Rosemary could only focus on the sick and dying. Their cheekbones protruded sharply from their faces and their bodies looked as if they had been hollowed out. They had to be supported by a friend as they shuffled slowly forward. Their clothes hung loosely over their bodies, and they carried with them, in the spaces between their skin and their clothes, a sense of vacancy - of empty places that needed to be filled. It was as if Rosemary was looking into her future. She decided that she needed to learn how to take better care of herself. Rosemary immediately joined the line and picked up her first batch of ARVs.

Whenever she fell sick, Rosemary feared the worst. She was afraid that if she died nobody would take care of her children. Sam's family rejected Rosemary completely. They wanted nothing to do with her or the children. Some days she felt too weak to get out of bed. The medicines often made her feel sick and she was always tired, but Rosemary had no choice but to struggle through every difficulty and hope that she could make it through the day. Many women in the neighbourhood were suffering just like her. She saw how they relied on men to bring food to their tables. One of Rosemary's neighbours juggled four boyfriends in her efforts to survive. Each man would bring groceries and money when they came to spend the night. Many other women found themselves in the same situation. Some of them resorted to standing in dark corners of the city and renting out their bodies to strangers for a few hours. Life was very difficult for Rosemary, but she never compromised herself in that way. Rosemary always believed that if she was given another opportunity she could still make something good of her life.

A New Beginning

One day Rosemary ran into Astilda, a friend from her neighbourhood who was also an HIV+ widow. Astilda mentioned that she had just signed up to enrol in the Living Hope program, and she suggested that Rosemary should join her.

Rosemary was sceptical. She found it hard to believe that Living Hope was willing to provide food and clothes for free, and that they made regular home visits to check up on the women enrolled in the program. Rosemary had raised her hopes on so many occasions. Several times she had paid cash for the opportunity to sign up for programs that had promised jobs and assistance for vulnerable people like her. But her money had been stolen and the organisations never delivered on their promises. Rosemary knew that she could trust a few of her close friends at church, but every experience with a charitable organisation had left her disappointed and bitter. Still, Astilda convinced Rosemary that it was worth her time to talk to Jolly, a Living Hope social worker, who lived in the neighbourhood.

When Rosemary arrived at Jolly's door she was greeted with a huge, friendly smile. Jolly welcomed Rosemary into her home and began to learn about Rosemary's struggles. Rosemary told her everything. Jolly had a warm and comforting spirit and she did not look down at Rosemary with judgment or condescension. Rosemary felt an immediate and unexpected peace. She filled in an application form and, as she was leaving, she asked if she could bring her friends to meet Jolly. Then she ran straight to the homes of her friends, Idah and Angela, and told them they had to sign up too.

"I'm a lady of responsibility. I'm HIV+,
but I'm not afraid. I'm confident. I
need to look after the children and work,
because I have a future."

- ROSEMARY BIRUNGI

A few days later, Jolly and a team from Living Hope visited Rosemary at her shack in the swamps. It was the first time anybody had visited her at her humble home. Rosemary felt that her life was beginning to turn around. A few weeks later Rosemary started her first day in the tailoring department at the Living Hope Centre in Kampala. At first she lacked confidence and she wanted to give up.

She had a hard time learning how to use the sewing machine and she couldn't understand the patterns that her instructors gave her. But as she looked around, she saw Rita, a lady that she recognised from her community. Rita also looked confused and a little lost, and Rosemary understood that she was not alone in her struggle. When Rosemary approached Rita during their morning tea break she learnt that it was Rita's first day too. They instantly bonded, and a real friendship was formed. Rosemary found some extra work for Rita, and Rita stopped by Rosemary's house to make sure she was eating well and taking her medicines.

The ladies at Living Hope were kind and encouraging, but as Rosemary struggled with her assignments each day, she continued to wonder if she was good enough. After a week, she went home and told Pauline that she was ready to quit. Her daughter smiled, and then said that she would not allow Rosemary to give up so easily. Pauline told her mother to go to bed, and insisted that in the morning she had to go back to Living Hope to try again. As Rosemary walked to work the next morning she stopped by her church and asked her pastor to pray for her. If she was going to master her sewing machine, Rosemary thought, she would need some miraculous intervention.

Living With Purpose

Slowly, Rosemary began to understand her craft. She found a natural rhythm as she worked the pedal on the sewing machine. As the wheels spun into motion she became less clumsy and she no longer feared the needle would sew her fingers together. She graduated to more complicated patterns. First she made a simple tablecloth, and then she made an apron. When she finally made a handbag that passed the Living Hope quality control test, she couldn't believe that she had succeeded. She turned it around in her hands, and hung it from her shoulder. She stood in front of the mirror and admired her reflection. In just a few short weeks she had blossomed. Her confidence began to soar. She made friends, and began to feel that she was living the kind of life that she was proud of. Her children stopped by the workshop after school and observed her from the window. When they came in, she showed them her work, and they were proud of their mother. They gave Rosemary a cheeky look and teased her, asking if it was really her who made these beautiful things.

Rosemary began to enjoy her work at Living Hope. She learned to raise the expectations she had for herself, and she learned how to pursue excellence. She learned that, while her challenges had brought to her a great deal of misery, they had also given her the opportunity to improve herself. She began to trust the other women in the tailoring department. She listened to the testimonies of some of her instructors, like Becky and Viola, and she understood that she too was capable of great things. They had overcome the same challenges, the same hardships, and now they were confident, strong women. They spoke up for those vulnerable women who couldn't speak for themselves. They were women of action. They intervened when necessary. They demonstrated Jesus' character by being obedient to his commandment to love as He loved.

Rosemary always believed that, if given the chance, she could pull herself out of her troubles. She just needed a helping hand, to balance and to guide her, as she navigated her way through her swamp. Poverty, HIV infection, loneliness and exhaustion had all held her back. Like the rain, which deposited sewerage, mud and trash in Rosemary's shack at the bottom of the valley, these challenges left sediments of doubt, confusion, and dejection that accumulated and left Rosemary inundated and immobile. It was as if she was fighting back a persistent flood, and was barely able to stay afloat.

Living Hope gave Rosemary what she needed most – another chance, and an opportunity to regain control of her life. It was the practical assistance that made the biggest difference to Rosemary. When she needed help to feed her children, Living Hope gave her food rations. When her baby fell sick, Living Hope provided Rosemary with the resources to get medical attention. Living Hope taught her a skill, and provided her with a way to earn a living. This stability, this predictability, allowed Rosemary to focus on rebuilding the foundation of her life.

As she put into practice the things that she learned at Living Hope, Rosemary began to succeed at last. When she graduated from the discipleship program, Living Hope gave Rosemary a small loan and she was able to reopen her canteen. Once again, she sells food, drinks and snacks from her porch. In this way, Rosemary is now able to supplement her income as a tailor at the Living Hope workshop in Kampala. Now, she earns enough to rent a small home for her family. She no longer has to live in the swamp. Her children are healthy and they all go to good schools. Rosemary has purpose and direction, and she has become an example to those who once thought that she had wasted her life.

MARY FIONA AKELLO
HEART OF A SERVANT, HANDS OF A NURSE

"But those who wait upon God get fresh strength.
They spread their wings and soar like eagles, They run and don't
get tired, they walk and don't lag behind."
- Isaiah 40:31

The sun had just risen over the Borassus palms on the gentle hills around Gulu town. The dew settled over the grass and the air was still morning fresh. Mary Fiona Akello was often the first to arrive at the Living Hope clinic. It was just a small room with a large open door, two desks and a shelf. By the time her colleagues arrived at the centre, Mary Fiona would have cleaned the office and prepared the instruments for the doctor. If she was not in the clinic, they would find her mingling with the Living Hope ladies, greeting each of them with an infectious smile.

During the day, the women enrolled in the Living Hope program would sit on a bench across a grassy pathway and wait for their turn to see a medical attendant. All day long, Mary Fiona would wholeheartedly tend to the needs of her patients. On a busy day the medical team would see as many as 30 ladies. Mary Fiona would give them their medicines, treat their wounds and injuries and organise the dispensary.

Most of the ladies at Living Hope have experienced a certain degree of indifference, neglect and sometimes stigma from nurses that they have visited. This is because many medical professionals in Uganda have grown accustomed to the prestige of their positions. But Nurse Mary Fiona was different. Her patients didn't have to hide anything about their illness, or feel silly about asking simple questions about their health. Mary Fiona understood that most of the ladies never finished elementary school and she saw it as her duty to provide them with simple answers. To their many questions she would answer them as to how they could prevent the diseases that were common amongst them and their children. She never discriminated or made them feel small. She understood them, and the ladies appreciated that she treated them with respect and dignity. Mary Fiona was approachable and friendly and she listened to their concerns, encouraged them, prayed with them and tended to their needs.

One day, when a lady called Eunice lost consciousness and collapsed just inside the gates of the Living Hope Centre; Mary Fiona ran to pick her up and rushed her to the hospital. The first person Eunice saw when she opened her eyes was Mary Fiona, sitting on the side of her bed smiling down at her. She told Eunice what had happened to her and let her know that she was very sick, but that she should put her trust in God and feel encouraged. Mary Fiona returned to work, but dropped by the hospital to see Eunice on her way home in the afternoon. Eunice stayed at the hospital that night but no family members came to visit her. Mary Fiona came by in the morning and brought some bread and juice for Eunice. She gave Eunice some money to get lunch and promised to be back later in the afternoon. When Eunice's cousin finally arrived, Mary Fiona encouraged her to be good to Eunice and reminded her that Eunice needed the love and support of her family.

For those who knew Mary Fiona, this wasn't unusual. She was known for the way she treated people with love and care. She was full of hope, and eager to give the best of herself to serve others. She brought with her an air of peace and the Living Hope ladies fed off of her optimism. When they were sick and frightened, she knew how to calm their fears.

Dreams

Mary Fiona was the second-last born in a family of 11 brothers and sisters. When she was 10 years old, her mother died. Fulfilling her mother's last wishes, Miriam, Mary Fiona's older sister took her in. Miriam was 27 years old, a single mother of three who worked a full-time job at the Bank of Uganda in Gulu. She became a mother to her two youngest sisters and she loved them as if they were her own daughters.

Mary Fiona was a brilliant student; she was the best in her class in Gulu Primary Public School and was offered a scholarship by the District Council. Miriam continued supporting her throughout her education, but when Mary Fiona was 18 years old, before she could enter Grade 10, she got pregnant and had to drop out of school.

She gave birth to a baby girl and named her Cesconia Abalo. Mary Fiona thought that she had missed her opportunity to finish high school but Miriam saw so much potential in Mary Fiona that she encouraged her to complete her studies.

Their father was a doctor's assistant and, ever since she was a little girl, Mary Fiona dreamed of one day becoming a doctor. Miriam believed her sister could accomplish her goals because she was dedicated, caring and very intelligent. So Miriam looked after young Cesconia while Mary Fiona finished her education. With the help of her sister, Mary Fiona finally graduated from high school in 1998 and she decided to train as a nurse. When she heard of a course being offered in the nearby town of Lira, Mary Fiona travelled to spend the weekend with an aunt who lived there.

Seasons of Torment

An interview was scheduled for the following Monday and she was excited and nervous about this opportunity. However, during the weekend she began to feel unwell. Usually Mary Fiona was a quiet, reserved girl and spoke only when she had something to say, but she became easily agitated, even aggressive. She started muttering things inaudibly to herself, eventually working herself into an animated frenzy. Now, she couldn't stop talking, loudly expressing an endless train of random and abstract thoughts and it was impossible for her aunt to understand what Mary Fiona was trying to communicate. She was becoming violent and angry, so her aunt called Miriam.

When Miriam arrived she found Mary Fiona responding aggressively to any instructions. Telling her to calm down seemed to make matters worse. She was out of control. When Miriam rushed her to the hospital, the doctors had no idea what to do, as there was no mental health unit in the area. The doctor decided to give her a sedative, but as Mary Fiona was tall and strong, he feared that she would attack him when she saw him approaching her with a needle. They decided to take her to the police station. She was locked up and the prisoners in her cell restrained her. When they had tied her down the medics sedated her.

Mary Fiona stayed in the prison cell for almost two weeks. Miriam stayed by her side and together they listened to Uganda's October 9th Independence Day celebrations and stared at the grim walls of the prison cell. Outside, people were drinking and feasting, music blared and fireworks illuminated the night sky, while Miriam sat and wondered what could possibly be happening to her younger sister. How could she help her?

Eventually the warden told Miriam to take Mary Fiona back to the hospital. The doctors were still unable to help; they didn't know what was happening to her. Miriam escorted Mary Fiona home to Gulu feeling exhausted and afraid. Soon Mary Fiona ran wild and uncontrollable. Miriam couldn't make her stay at home and when she disappeared, as she often did, it was impossible to keep track of her whereabouts. Five months later, almost as suddenly as it had started, Mary Fiona recovered and returned to her senses, so Miriam took her to see a specialist in psychiatric disorders at Gulu Hospital. The doctor met with Mary Fiona on several occasions and eventually diagnosed her with Bipolar Affective Disorder. Her condition often manifested itself in manic phases and she would become, excited, anxious and irritable. He prescribed a medication for Mary Fiona that he hoped would stabilise her mood. However, it only worked sporadically and she soon began experiencing new episodes of mental instability.

"She was full of hope, and eager to give the best of herself to serve others."

74

In the small, closely connected community of Gulu stories began to surface of Mary Fiona's behaviour. Someone said they saw her break the neighbour's windows. Another person said they found her throwing rocks at a business in town. For Mary Fiona, the headaches were unbearable and her thoughts were always racing; she had insomnia and could go for days without sleeping. During the night she would sing loudly or talk incessantly. She was often restless, excited and full of energy. Occasionally she would start to improve and try to find ways to make her dream of becoming a nurse a reality. For a full month her disposition changed, she became herself again, but before she had a chance to begin her training, she relapsed.

Again, Mary Fiona began wandering aimlessly around town at night. People reported that they had seen her roaming the streets in her young daughter's clothes. Sometimes she walked through town naked. She became completely wild, and someone decided to restrain her by chaining her naked to a lamppost. She didn't always remember what happened to her during her manic phases and she wasn't in control of her actions. Miriam sat up at night, like a concerned mother. She was terrified of the fate her sister faced when she slept outside. To make matters worse, LRA rebels often raided the city and Miriam would sometimes listen to the sound of bullets as they unleashed terror on the community. Children were being abducted, women tortured and mutilated. Anything could have happened to Mary Fiona.

One morning Mary Fiona returned home and even though most nights were a blur, she knew she had been raped. Because of her condition few people seemed to care and it was impossible to know how often men took advantage of her. Miriam was desperate and knew that she had to act. She no longer believed the medicine the doctors had prescribed was working and was convinced that evil spirits were tormenting her sister. Miriam resorted to desperate measures. She professed to be a Christian and regularly attended church, but still Miriam began to search for the best witch doctor she could find. She made the five-hour journey to Mbale, in eastern Uganda, to meet him. Miriam was tired, distressed and eager to find a solution to her sister's torment. She, like many in her culture, believed that there are many unseen spirits that wield power over people and control events in their lives. Miriam became convinced that only a very powerful witch doctor had authority over the spirits that tormented her sister and she was willing to pay whatever price he demanded. Many of her family and friends had visited these witch doctors and paid enormous amounts of money for a ritual they believed would ensure they enjoyed health, prosperity or even revenge. It was a last resort; a concession that she had no control over the events and actions that could heal her sister. In her desperation she willingly submitted to this merchant of the dark arts.

Outside the witch doctor's hut, a chicken was slaughtered. Its head fell to the ground; its blood splattered over the red dust, and the chicken's body quivered wildly in front of them. Mary Fiona sat in a hut with her arms extended as the "doctor" brewed a mixture of herbs from his garden. He approached Mary Fiona, made a few clean cuts on her arms and applied the concoction over the incision. Then he burned the rest of the ingredients and fanned the smoke so that it surrounded Mary Fiona and he told her to inhale the burnt offering. Miriam paid the man handsomely and returned home, hoping her earnest supplication to the spirits would heal her sister, but nothing changed. Mary Fiona continued experiencing erratic mood changes and Miriam was angry and embarrassed that she had fallen for such a scam.

A Devoted Sister

When she told a friend at church about all of her efforts to help her sister, Miriam was advised to entirely commit her life to Christ and to pray for Mary Fiona's healing. This, said Miriam's friend, was the only solution to her problem. At that moment Miriam decided to make a radical transformation in her life. No longer would she just attend church as part of a weekly, cultural routine. She decided to devote herself completely to God and submit her troubles to Him.

She began attending church more regularly and brought Mary Fiona along with her. She held fellowship in her home and she prayed over Mary Fiona every day. They fasted together. After work, Miriam went to church and prayed fervently. It was a long and difficult process, but she didn't give up. With the combination of prayer and the medicine, gradually Mary Fiona's condition improved. She became calm and focused, and began to understand that she was being healed. She started sleeping more and talking less. Miriam and Mary Fiona continued praying and together they grew in their faith.

Mary Fiona had no recollection of her torments, and it was difficult for her to comprehend that the dark and indiscernible silences that cut gaps in her memory were filled with such horrors. She had lost days, weeks and months of her life. To fill in the blank spaces of her memory she had to rely on what other people told her about herself, but as she began to piece together her story she felt ashamed and embarrassed. She felt like she was a burden to her sister and so she felt insignificant and incapable. Miriam continued to encourage and believe in her sister. She noticed that Mary Fiona was improving each day and so Miriam relentlessly poured love into her sister's life. Mary Fiona responded by feeding off of her sister's kindness and she steadily improved. She was being transformed by an indescribable and holy love. God was using Miriam to bring healing to her sister. Mary Fiona began to recognise her own value. She no longer felt paralyzed by insecurity and so she applied for a position to train as a nurse at Lacor School of Nursing and she was accepted.

One day, Mary Fiona heard that the hospital was testing people for HIV/AIDS, and she decided that she was ready to know her status. When she found out that she was HIV+ she was heartbroken. Again Miriam encouraged Mary Fiona and advised her that if she took the ARV drugs that she would be able to survive and live a long, fruitful life. There was one man, she said, who had lived more than 30 years after discovering he had HIV. Mary Fiona gathered her strength and decided to make the most of the life in front of her.

Miriam supported her throughout her education and helped her with Cesconia's school fees. Mary Fiona helped her sister at home; cooking, cleaning and gardening. To Miriam, Mary Fiona was never a burden. She filled her life with joy and was always ready to listen to her sister's concerns. She was a true friend and it was a joy to have her around. If Miriam ever fell sick, Mary Fiona would care for her and tend to her every need with generosity and selflessness.

Finally Mary Fiona completed her three-year nursing course and was offered an internship at a hospital six miles away from her home. She volunteered there for several years, riding her bike early in the morning and coming back home late at night. It was a difficult journey to take every single day. More than ever, she wanted to serve God by helping others and after discovering her HIV status she realised that she wanted to help women who were just like her. Despite the hardships of her past, she had benefitted from the love of a family that was loyal and supportive. Her sister never gave up on her. She had seen how some women who came to the hospital had been rejected by their friends and families. Nobody wanted to touch or care for them because they had HIV. Some of them suffered alone and nobody came to visit them. They died feeling isolated, abandoned and entirely worthless.

Finding Purpose

When she heard that Living Hope was looking for a volunteer nurse, Mary Fiona knew that she was the perfect candidate. She understood the stigma and the feelings of inferiority that the Living Hope women endured because she was just like them. She began to realise that her story allowed her to approach and love these women in a way that others could not. In May, 2009, Mary Fiona began working at the Living Hope Centre in Gulu. When she shared her story with all of the women at morning devotions one day, they responded by opening up to her. They understood that she was one of them.

She regarded every task that she performed as an act of worship to God. She gave the best of herself to her work, and she began to recognise that she was part of something bigger than herself.

Now she was living a life that had purpose. She had a vision and so she had hope, and this hope gave her strength, despite her sickness. Through her work she became a blessing to countless vulnerable women.

Miriam would often find Mary Fiona in the kitchen packing supper for a Living Hope lady who didn't have any family members to care for her. She would sometimes stay at the hospital for days on end where she was the only person there to comfort and care for a sick and dying patient. If the ladies were too weak to come to the Living Hope Centre, Mary Fiona would join the medical team to make home visits and would often repeat the journey alone a few days later to monitor the progress of her patients. She often had to travel for several hours to carry out these check ups, but she never seemed to tire of her work.

As she attended the daily devotionals, and as she listened in on the discipleship classes across the yard, Mary Fiona learned that God loved her. She began to understand that her past did not have to define her. She noticed that many women were being transformed as they were shown how to deal with their traumas, how to forgive, and how to love themselves. Mary Fiona began to deal with her own past and she continued to heal. A few months after joining Living Hope as a volunteer, Mary Fiona was offered a permanent position at the clinic. She couldn't contain her excitement and she rushed to tell the news to Celia, a friend and colleague at the clinic. She told Celia that she was so happy to be earning a steady income because now she could tithe regularly with her own money at her church. After work she ran to share the news with Miriam. "Now you will finally be able to relax," she said to Miriam. "You don't have to stress anymore. I can pay my daughter's school fees; I'll be able to start my own business."

Mary Fiona began to develop a vision for her future together with her daughter. She developed a plan to open her own pharmacy and wanted to buy a plot of land that she could farm. She was dreaming big. She began taking over more of the responsibilities at home and helping Miriam with bills. But in June, 2011, Mary Fiona fell sick. She had started to lose weight and was looking pale. Miriam came home and found her shivering under four blankets in the middle of the sweltering afternoon heat. Her immune system was failing and she was admitted to Lacor hospital on Wednesday July 13th with a blood infection. Every evening after work, Miriam went to visit her sister. Their cousin, who worked at the hospital, gave them regular updates. When Celia went to see her, she was doing much better - she was walking and eating. On Sunday some friends came by after church and they sat with the sisters in the visitor's lounge and braided Mary Fiona's hair. They prayed together and Mary Fiona felt loved and encouraged. She never let her beautiful smile slip from her face. She died four days later on July 21st, 2011.

A few days later more than 100 people squeezed into two buses in front of the Living Hope Centre in Gulu and travelled to Mary Fiona's village to bury her. There they celebrated her life with a crowd of people who had assembled to remember her. There were family members, friends, nurses she had trained with, colleagues from the hospitals where she had volunteered, and Living Hope ladies, some of whose lives she had helped to save. Mary Fiona was so remarkable because she overcame the challenges that could easily have destroyed her. She experienced a unique and isolating pain, and yet she was transformed by love.

Some of those, who once might have said that she was cursed, now gathered at her grave to recognise that Mary Fiona was a blessing. She exemplified courage, determination and joy. Her life was a gift to those who knew her and she was elevated amongst her peers because she used the power of her testimony to glorify God and to edify others.

The Living Hope Centre in Gulu, Uganda

"We are not giving them something new; we are restoring. What we are doing is saying, 'God did not make you this broken, wounded, incapable person. When you were in the womb, God made you beautiful. He made you strong, joyful and capable.' Circumstances have taken that away, and we are here to restore it."

- CHRISTINE LUTARA, TEAM LEADER
LIVING HOPE, GULU

FLORENCE NANFUKA
BEAUTY BEYOND ANY PRICE

"I live in the high and holy places, but also with the low-spirited, the spirit-crushed, And what I do is put new spirit in them, get them up and on their feet again." - Isaiah 57:15

Florence stood by the window of her aunt's house and gently pulled aside a corner of the curtain to discreetly watch what was happening outside. There were four men standing pompously, each one of them dressed in their finest kanzu* and wearing a round embroidered cap. It appeared as if they were headed to the mosque, but judging by the manner in which they were discussing some piece of solemn business, it looked like a transaction was taking place and they had arrived at the home of Florence's aunt to collect something. One man, who seemed to be their leader, wore a certain air of entitlement and confidently stood at the centre of the group. He said nothing yet he commanded the respect of his peers. She watched his hands fumble with a handkerchief and then he folded it and began to wipe the sweat from his forehead. Silently he waited in the burning heat of the midday sun.

Florence took a deep breath and tried to hold back her tears. Her throat was dry and her heart raced as she wiped the sweat from her palms onto her dress.

*Kanzu: a traditional robe worn by men in many parts of Uganda.

She composed herself, lifted her head and shoulders proudly and turned to meet her aunt's threatening glance. Her aunt signalled Florence to the door and reminded her of the consequences if she refused, for a third time, to marry the man who was waiting outside for her.

Florence stepped timidly through the door and as her eyes adjusted to the bright light shining on the man, who was to be her husband, she began to make out his features. Her heart sank like a stone. This time there would be no escape. Her aunt was a powerful witch doctor and even though her family were Muslims they all feared this woman. Florence had managed to resist her aunt's insistence that she marry on two previous occasions, and when Florence refused to go through with the arrangements that her aunt had made for her, the men were left humiliated and had returned to their other wives, trophy-less. Now her aunt told her that if she refused again, she would put a curse on Florence, and even if she should run away, Florence would die. She was terrified and she believed her aunt's threats. Florence was 16 years old when she became the fourth wife of a 40 year-old man.

She was a reluctant bride who had run out of options. There was nowhere else to go and she owned nothing. Florence had tried to make a life for herself away from her family, but she was still a child and she had struggled just to survive. So she was forced to return to live within the clutches of her aunt's cruel vengeance.

Now she was entirely dependent upon people who did not care for her and who thought of her as a burden. The only way for her father, brothers and aunt to get rid of her was to marry her off. Some older man, one who had grown tired of his other wives and was looking for a more youthful attraction would not be able to resist Florence.

Oppressed

Her father had done very little to support Florence during her childhood. When she was only eight months old her mother died and, because her father had two other wives and 13 children to care for, Florence was sent to live with her father's sister. Her aunt owned several properties and did reasonably well from the rent she collected, but really earned her living by practicing traditional medicine. She spent her days creating herbal medicines to help women give birth or to heal common illnesses. Sometimes she would tell Florence to gather and crush the herbs needed to create her traditional concoction.

The aunt lived in Kalerwe, a suburb north of Kampala. The entire area was located around a swampy valley. When it rained the water would flow down the surrounding hills and carry with it piles of garbage and excrement that would collect in Florence's neighbourhood. The streets and alleys of the market flooded and became soft with mud and the filth of the city. The narrow paths between the slanted and decrepit stalls became slippery trails covered in waste from the market, choked with plastic bags and rotting vegetables. When the rain poured down at night Florence would curl up in her bed, made of grass-filled sacks, stacked on top of each other, and she would pray that the water wouldn't rise and submerge her makeshift mattress.

Her life was hard, and Florence deeply regretted that her mother had died before Florence could speak or walk. She missed her mother, even though she could recall no memories of her and she craved for a warm embrace or a kind word. She longed to be told that she was valuable; that she brought happiness to somebody; she imagined her mother supporting and lovingly encouraging her as she grew up. Her aunt was a cold, intimidating woman whose glance was enough to send the children running. Florence was the one she scorned the most. She was the youngest and yet she was responsible for all the household chores. She had to carry water, fetch firewood, cook and clean and she had to wake up early to dig in the garden.

The best hours of her day were spent at school. Here she excelled and received the encouragement that she didn't get at home. Her science teacher, recognizing her intelligence and her patience, put Florence in charge of tutoring the students who were falling behind in their work. She joined every club, and participated in every extra-curricular activity that she could. Florence was a talented athlete, and loved to sing and dance. She did anything that ensured that she was away from home for as long as possible. She made many friends and she thrived. Florence would return home to her aunt's harsh words and a list of chores that she could never complete to her aunt's satisfaction. She felt like a constant disappointment and these thoughts were reinforced every day as she endured an endless assault of criticism that tore down any confidence that she built up when at school.

When Florence reached Grade 6 her father stopped paying the school fees and she had to drop out of school. It was in these moments, when life's big decisions were made for her and she was given no say in the matter, that Florence ached for her mother's affection. She imagined that her mother would have intervened, that she would have protected her daughter and encouraged her potential.

Beyond Hope

Now, Florence had no prospects or skills to rely on, and soon after she turned 16, her aunt arranged a marriage for her. The first time that happened, Florence had returned home and found a group of strangers who were waiting for her aunt. Florence greeted them and welcomed them into the house. She assumed that they had come to solicit the witch doctor's services. Her aunt took Florence aside and, spitefully whispering in her ear, told Florence that the visitors were here for her. It was time for Florence to get married, she said, and if Florence refused she would have to find somewhere else to live. Florence decided instantly.

She ran to a neighbour, a lady who rented a house from her aunt, and begged her for a few shillings so that she could pay for a taxi to visit her father. Florence was an obedient and gentle girl and many of her aunt's tenants felt compassion for her. They observed from afar how her aunt mistreated her and, whenever Florence came to them, they were willing to help where they could.

Florence gathered the money she needed and went to see her father, but when she arrived he confronted her. How dare she disrespect her aunt and refuse to marry? How dare she run away?

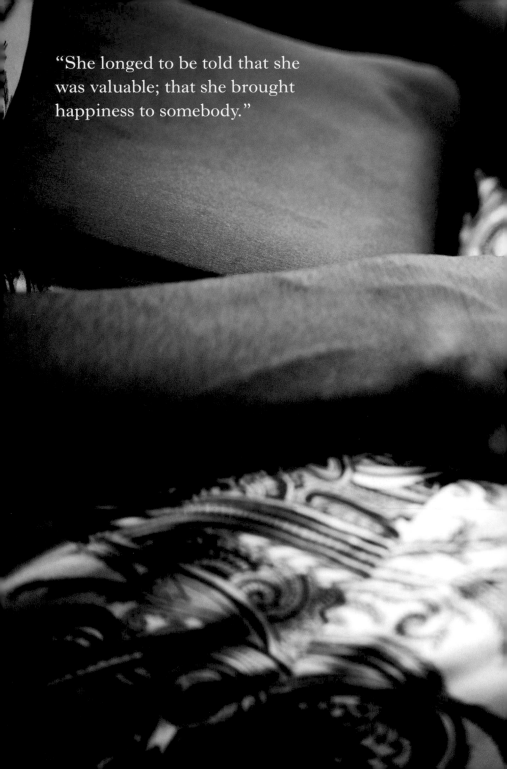

"She longed to be told that she was valuable; that she brought happiness to somebody."

Her father gave her two options; she could return to her aunt, apologise and marry the man her aunt had chosen for her; or she could "carry soil" - she would be cursed and disowned; her name would be tarnished and she would never be allowed to return to the family.

Florence chose to "carry soil." With the little money she had left, she returned to the neighbour, who had previously helped her, and asked if she could sleep there. But as soon as her aunt learned that Florence was staying with one of her tenants, she threatened to evict the woman unless Florence returned home. Reluctantly, the neighbour agreed, and though she felt sorry for Florence, made her leave. Florence was destroyed. She had nowhere to go and no money in her pockets. She had no skills or opportunities to make a living. Her only prospect was to return to her aunt's home and continue to serve her, or to find another person to depend on by getting married.

She returned to her aunt's home and continued working for her. But her aunt's plans for Florence didn't change. She found another man for her to marry. Again, Florence boldly refused and the party of men scattered. Her aunt was furious and was determined to get rid of her. At the third attempt, driven by fear and despondence, Florence gave in. She sobbed as she stood in front of a group of men that she had never met, as they negotiated with her family over her price. Her eldest brother was there to give her hand away in marriage. The local sheik performed the ceremony and after a few handshakes and a small payment, Florence became a wife. She was sold for 200 shillings, which at the time was the price of a cheap pair of shoes.

That same day she packed her bags, said goodbye to her family, and moved into her new home. When she arrived she was met by the proud glances of her co-wives as her husband's friends and family danced to the sounds of the harp. They beat drums and tambourines and there was a feast prepared to celebrate the arrival of another bride. Her husband was a rich man. His house had nine rooms, a spacious living space and a kitchen, which they all shared. The property had a large garden and each wife had a section on which they could grow vegetables. But Florence found no comfort in her surroundings.

Sinking into Bitterness

She did not love her husband and his other wives were threatened by her. Many were from a different part of the country and she didn't speak their language. At first the other wives whispered amongst themselves, so that Florence couldn't understand them. Soon, even their children were insulting and mistreating her, to her face. She felt isolated and excluded, but most of all she felt betrayed by her family. Given the chance, Florence knew that she could have excelled at many things, but the course of her life had been determined by people who only wanted to get rid of her. She became distant and indifferent before sinking into a long, deep bitterness.

Florence lived in her husband's house for 15 years; she gave birth to five children, but her husband soon took a new wife and lost interest in her. Still, when he had tired of his other wives and mistresses, he would come and stay with Florence.

Florence hated her life. So many women came and left, and she felt worthless to her husband. He put a roof over her head, but he didn't pay her children's school fees, or give her any money to buy food. The only way she could support herself was by growing potatoes in the garden and selling them on the side of the road. This is how she fed her children.

When her husband fell sick, his other wives abandoned him, and Florence was the only one who stayed behind to take care of him. She thought of leaving too, but she knew she couldn't cope with five children to take care of. Instead she tried to nurse her husband back to health but his condition deteriorated steadily. Eventually she took him to the hospital where they discovered that he had HIV. Florence felt a stabbing pain in her heart and immediately knew that she was also infected with the virus. When the doctor confirmed her status, Florence wept for her children. She wondered if she would live long enough to see them grow. Would they survive? What kind of people would they become?

Soon her husband died, and when Florence left the hospital and returned to her home, she found her in-laws waiting to repossess all of the dead man's property. The land, the house and everything in it belonged to them, they said, and they told Florence to take her children and leave their property. She managed to pack a blanket and two bed sheets, but her in-laws inspected her every move and followed her steps through the house to make sure she took nothing else.

Her husband had been dead for only a few days and now Florence was homeless, abandoned and stripped of any hope for her future. Her children were hungry, but she had nothing to feed them. She pondered her options, and when she understood that her only choice was to return to the home of the aunt who had sold her into marriage for the price of a pair of shoes, she sobbed inconsolably. Now a widow, she felt ashamed, humiliated and totally helpless. She wanted to protect her children from the pain she had experienced as a little girl, but now she was taking them back to the place where her nightmares began. Florence gathered the courage to return to her aunt's house and hoped that she would be met with compassion.

Out of duty, her aunt reluctantly opened her doors to Florence and her children. She allowed them to stay in her house, but she showed neither care nor respect. She knew that Florence was HIV+ and so she mistreated and marginalised them. She refused to share her food or allow Florence to cook in her home. She believed that by sharing a fork or a spoon Florence could transmit the disease, so she forbade Florence from using anything from her kitchen. Again, her neighbours were kind to her and gave her some money and allowed her to borrow one of their cooking pots. Florence bought some plantain and cut some leaves from a banana tree in the neighbours garden and made some matooke and peanut sauce. When it was ready she put the pot on her head and carried it to sell at the market. In the afternoon she came back home with enough money to buy her own pot and to repay what her neighbour had loaned her.

Every day she went to market with some matooke and peanut sauce and returned with just enough money to feed her children. She couldn't afford to send them to school or to rent a place of her own so she began to look for other opportunities.

When she heard of an organisation that was raising awareness about HIV and providing ARVs for people living with the disease she joined their drama team as a volunteer. They travelled throughout the district encouraging people to take their HIV tests, so that they could know their status. For the first time since she was forced into marriage, Florence felt that she could do something good with her life. At the same time, she hoped that somebody would help her find a job, or sponsor her children's education. Every day she laboured to earn enough so that her family could eat supper, but sometimes they went hungry.

Destitute

Some time later, her aunt died and Florence was chased out of the home by her cousins. There was nowhere else for Florence to go. No family or friend offered to keep her for a few nights. Everybody she knew abandoned her and left her at the mercy of the city streets. She wrapped her few belongings in a blanket and slung them over her back and, together with her children, she walked the streets of Kampala for hours, scouting a location to settle for the night. She collected cardboard from trash heaps and alleyways.

As businesses closed for the day and people journeyed home, Florence sat with her children on the sidewalk. Together, they extended their hands and begged. She felt ashamed, but she knew that if she did not humble herself in this way, her children would not eat. With the money one kind passersby tossed into her hand she could afford a plate of cornmeal from the market. They ate and waited for the market to empty.

Slowly the vendors began packing their things and covering their stalls. Once it was dark, Florence found a lonely and quiet corner and timidly began to lay out the pieces of cardboard she had collected. However, a group of menacing men came by and harassed her. They said she needed permission to sleep on their streets and forced her to move. She retreated to another alley and spread the cardboards and sheets to create a bed for the children. She reserved a tiny corner for herself, letting her children spread out over the rest. Tears streamed silently down her face as she watched her children fall asleep. Florence didn't need to sleep to be visited by her nightmares. Her entire life, every incident, every relationship, every broken dream, every meaningless thing that was hers, was there with her - laid out on the dirt. She felt the heat of the day radiating from her cheeks and she was broken.

When she recalled her memories all she could remember was pain, spite and rejection. All of her life she had just wanted an opportunity, a chance to be respectable. She knew now that she was nothing. As she surveyed the compilation of her life, all that she saw was emptiness and her children. She reached out her arms and as they slept she wrapped them all in her love and she decided to stay alive for them.

At dawn she woke her children and went to forage for food at the market. Before the vendors arrived at their stalls or the street cleaners came to sweep up the scraps from the day before, Florence rummaged through piles of rotting vegetables and garbage and searched under stalls hoping to find something for them to eat.

"I thought that I was a nobody. I had no identity. But through Living Hope, I discovered that I do have value and God loves me."

– FLORENCE NANFUKA

After feeding her children, Florence went to the drama club where she was a volunteer and shared her circumstances with some of the people she worked with, hoping that someone would be able to help her. Many listened and felt sorry for her, but nobody helped her. That night she slept at the public hospital. She lay down with her children on the filthy floor in a corridor of the busiest hospital in Kampala, surrounded by a throng of sick patients and crying infants.

The next day at the drama club, one lady noticed that Florence was exhausted and frail. She watched as the youngest child cried for something to eat, but Florence had nothing to give him. Fearing that something might happen to the little family on the street or that the children would get sick at the hospital she offered Florence a place to stay at her home.

Florence was overwhelmed. In her entire life she had rarely experienced an act of care or sympathy. This simple act of kindness rekindled a sense of hope in Florence's heart and gave her some courage. With a renewed strength she woke up the next morning and obtained permission to sell corn outside the building where the drama club met.

Soon Florence had earned enough to rent a small shack and she packed her belongings and moved with her children. For the first time in her life she was free. Her decisions were now her own and nobody was forcing her to do anything against her will. No longer must she tolerate the insults that were endlessly hurled at her by her family. She felt so proud. But soon her dream was crushed. She was unable to make enough money just by selling food on the street, and her landlord threatened to evict her. Again she began to feel inadequate, inferior and incapable. She started to believe again the lies her family had told her, and she wondered if her life was worth anything at all.

Discovering Her Value

On her way back from the drama club one day, Florence walked by a park where a pastor was preaching to a crowd. She felt compelled to stop and listen. Florence was dispirited by the possibility of once again ending up on the streets with her children. When the pastor finished his sermon, she approached him and poured out her heart. He felt compassion for her and allowed her to stay in the church while she saved enough to rent again. Every night she slept with her children in a corner of the church auditorium and prayed that she would find deliverance from her misery.

One day when Florence was at the clinic to collect her ARVs, the doctor told her that Living Hope was looking for HIV+ single mothers because they wanted to help them. When Florence first arrived at Living Hope she was reclusive. She felt insignificant even in the midst of all the other vulnerable women. Her life had been a succession of endless letdowns and disappointments, and so she didn't allow herself to believe that she could amount to anything at all.

Slowly, as she learned to read her Bible and was discipled by women who, just like her, had experienced terrible hardship and pain, she began to realise that there was hope. Had she seen these women boarding a taxi beside her, she would never believe that they too had HIV; that they too had been abandoned, neglected, abused.

Instead they were confident and overflowing with joy and fulfilment. They acknowledged the pain, which had dominated much of their lives, but they spoke with wisdom, and from their own personal understanding, of the capacity to change. The unifying element, the thing that made the difference for each of them, was that somebody, in obedience to an unscripted prompt, had shown them Jesus' perfect love. And so Florence too began to change. She began to believe that God loved her, and she began to understand her value. Her heart began to open up and she flourished. Soon she too began to encourage other women, and they were surprised because they only knew her to be shy and intimidated.

Now she was confident, and as she learned to sew and to make jewellery, she believed in her ability. She learned how to manage her money, how to save and to plan for her future and how to manage a small business. After two years at Living Hope, Florence graduated and was given a small loan to help her start her own business. Florence began to make her own jewellery and paper beads, which she sold in her community. A few months later she repaid her loan and began to save. Within a year she was able to buy her own small plot of land. Now she's dreaming of building a home for her children and she's confident that her grandchildren will grow to know her as a woman of strength, generosity and love.

LUCY LAKER
ESCAPE INTO HOPE

"I have it all planned out—plans to take care of you, not abandon you, plans to give you the future you hope for."
- Jeremiah 29:11

Joseph Kony inspected the display of recently abducted girls who were standing naked in front of him. One of them would be his newest wife, and because he was the leader of the Lord's Resistance Army, he was the first to choose from the line of young girls that he had sent his soldiers to kidnap. Lucy was barely 14 years old and, although she didn't show it, she was terrified. It was useless to dream that she could be like other teenage girls, studying hard, preparing herself for a career and working towards a dream. She could no longer afford the luxury of personal ambition. As she stood motionless, her neck and head held high and her dejected gaze fixed on some remote object, Lucy's future was being determined for her.

She trembled gently. Nobody here cared for her. They just wanted to use her for labour and for sex. Joseph Kony paced along the line of girls and without shame or guilt analyzed their every feature. Behind him another line had formed. LRA commanders queued up in order of their rank, leering at the girls and waiting their turn to select which one they wanted as their newest trophy wife.

Finally, Kony stopped in front of a girl called Susan, and grabbing her by the arm, he pulled her violently from the line. He dragged Susan away and told the other commanders to choose for themselves. These girls were his gift to them for their loyalty.

Sweat collected on Lucy's temples. Her heart was racing, blood rushed to her cheeks and she blushed at her humiliating exposure. She fought off her emotions and tried to contain her rage and embarrassment. But, moments earlier, a man that she had never met, performed a vulgar fertility ritual by rubbing oil over her bare breasts, and now she stood naked in front of a group of degenerate men. She felt stripped of all dignity and respect.

Abduction

Only a few days earlier, Lucy had been at home with her parents and sister when rebel soldiers raided her village in the middle of the night. Kony had given them instructions to find the prettiest girls and to bring them back so he could choose for himself a new wife. By the time the rebels broke down Lucy's door they had already abducted two other girls. One of them was Susan. Lucy's sister was quick to realise what was happening and she managed to escape, but Lucy was not so lucky. The rebels tied a rope around her waist and bound her to the other girls. When her mother, who was sleeping in another hut, heard the commotion she ran towards the men in a fit of fury. She was prepared to fight for Lucy's life, but she was outnumbered and easily overpowered by the rebels. They beat her violently and left her lying in the dirt wailing over the fate of her daughter.

LUCY LAKER

She watched as Lucy was dragged away from the comforts of her family through the cassava plantation that surrounded the homestead and disappeared into a sinister and unknown blackness.

The three girls were forced to walk for many hours until their abductors were confident that it was impossible for the girls to find their way home if they tried to escape. They stopped their march and laid down in the tall grass to sleep for a few hours. Lucy was exhausted from the terrors of her abduction and so she slept. When she awoke, her captors forced her and the other girls to carry heavy loads of beans, corn, salt and sugar on their backs. Their long march began again. Lucy didn't know where they were going or what was in store for her, but she feared the worst. Eventually the group arrived at a large encampment, a village that was crowded with people moving about in a frenzied haste. Many young girls were looking after groups of babies while the women and older girls were cooking and cleaning. In one area a group of soldiers huddled together in a circle and discussed some serious business. Close by, a group of children no older than 12 were shooting guns at a piece of paper that was hanging from a distant tree. A few uniformed soldiers watched over the boys and girls and instructed them on how to perfect their aim.

Lucy was taken to the house of a woman where she learned what was going to happen to her. She and the other girls would be taught how to take care of a rebel commander and, when they were ready, they would move into his house and become his property.

Shameful Selection

In a matter of days her training was complete. Together with the other recent abductees she was brought before Joseph Kony and his commanders and she became a wife. Lucy was chosen by a man who was more than twice her age. George Komakech was an important rebel leader, the second in command of the LRA rebellion and Joseph Kony's right-hand-man. He had led the raid on Lucy's village and targeted her because he was immediately attracted to her. From the moment he first saw Lucy he was determined to make her his fourth wife.

When Kony selected Susan, George Komakech, who was the next in line, fixed his gaze on Lucy and smiled haughtily. Then, with focus and purpose, he walked straight to Lucy and claimed her as his own. He did not ask her. He simply put his hand on her arm, took a hold of her and plucked her from the line of girls as if she were merchandise on display in a shop window. There was no ceremony or celebration. It was a simple transaction between a thief and his stolen object, and because Lucy was now his possession, he took her back to his home to treat her as he wished.

A few days later, Lucy's friend Susan ran away. She humiliated Joseph Kony by refusing to be his wife; so he sent his finest soldiers to hunt her down. They returned a few days later and paraded her blood-soaked clothes around the camp, boasting of how they killed Susan and stripped her before abandoning her corpse in the wilderness. She was 15 years old.

Lucy knew that it was useless to think of escaping. Instead she must learn to survive. But what would she do when George Komakech decided that it was time for Lucy to fulfill her obligations as a wife? If she refused to have sex with him she would be committing a serious offense and her punishment would be especially severe. To rape his wives was a commander's entitlement. A woman who was unwilling to submit to this treatment could be easily discarded and replaced, but such an offense would first be met with unrelenting vengeance and cruelty. And yet, the mere thought of escape was now intrinsically entwined with the story of Susan's brutal death and Lucy was convinced that if she were to run away she would meet the same end. At the very least, if she escaped and was caught she would be tortured.

Many re-captured girls were punished by mutilation - their ears, lips and noses were cut off with razor blades. Lucy had seen these girls when walking in the camp and when their eyes met she wanted to look away. But their disfiguration could not be ignored, and this was the intention. Now she faced a life-altering choice and time was quickly running out for her to decide - she could run and risk death, or she could stay and submit to the man who had destroyed her life. She decided to plan her escape.

A few days later, on Christmas day, the camp swarmed with people who were returning from villages where they had stolen goats, chickens and sugar. The women built fires in long lines and prepared, in stolen pots, a feast for the troops. The entire camp gathered in a circle to celebrate Christmas around a huge bonfire and, after feasting, Kony commanded one solider to turn up the radio. The warlord wanted to dance.

As the crowd joined Kony and danced for hours around the fire, Lucy sat alone in a shadow and thought about running away.

The conditions were perfect, she thought. The commanders were unusually distracted and entirely absorbed in dance. The blaring music would disguise any sound she might make as she escaped through the bushes and thick grass. She began to believe she could make it and slowly she began to work up her courage as she stared blankly into the raging fire. The men were dancing themselves into a frenzy. George Komakech was laughing with Joseph Kony and she watched them shake their bodies to the beat of the music. They were so content with themselves, so pleased with their murderous domination, so righteously superior. She must escape. She must run and not look back until she was home with her family. She felt an arm over her shoulder. She flinched and turned to see one of her co-wives. It was her turn to make her husband's bed.

While George mingled and feasted, Lucy went to his tent and prepared his bed for the night. When she had finished she quickly returned to her own tent and again turned her thoughts towards escape. But only a few minutes passed before George Komakech sent for Lucy. Tonight he was going to make their marriage official. Lucy understood his intentions and she panicked. She pleaded and protested, but her co-wife advised her not to reject her husband. George Komakech heard Lucy's voice and began calling for her, out loud.

Slowly, agonizingly, Lucy approached his tent. She was outraged and terrified. Escape was impossible. Only a few meters separated Lucy from George Komakech. When she got to his tent she fell to her knees on the ground outside, and then, slowly, she turned and sat in the dirt with her back towards him. She could not enter. Every impulse within her rejected an advance that would take her any closer to George Komakech. Lucy prayed for rescue, for any escape from this place. She pleaded and begged for release and she began to cry.

At first, she tried to hold back her tears, but once a few of them had been released, she could not contain the torrent that burst out of her. George Komakech called her again and commanded her to enter the tent, but Lucy gathered her courage and told him that she was a virgin. She begged him to let her sleep outside. She was paralyzed with fear. Her heart was pounding violently and she could feel her blood beating inside her head and rushing violently through her veins. She began to shake and her hands became tense and clenched themselves into tight fists. Her throat became dry and she tried to swallow.

George Komakech unleashed his fury. He rose from his bed and leapt viciously towards her. He threw open the tent flap and grabbed Lucy with one hand around her neck and a pistol aimed at her forehead. If she did not submit to him, if she did not obey his commands, he said, he was happy to kill her. Then he grabbed Lucy by the shirt and dragged her into his tent before wrestling her onto his bed. Lucy recoiled. She tried with all of her strength to resist George Komakech. She kicked and screamed in torment. He grabbed her by the throat, and strangling her until she couldn't fight any more, George Komakech raped Lucy. Outside the tent, Christmas music blared and Joseph Kony celebrated himself around the fire.

Nine months later Lucy was curled up in pain at a missionary clinic in Sudan. Her husband's troops had been stationed there and it was time for Lucy to give birth to her first child.

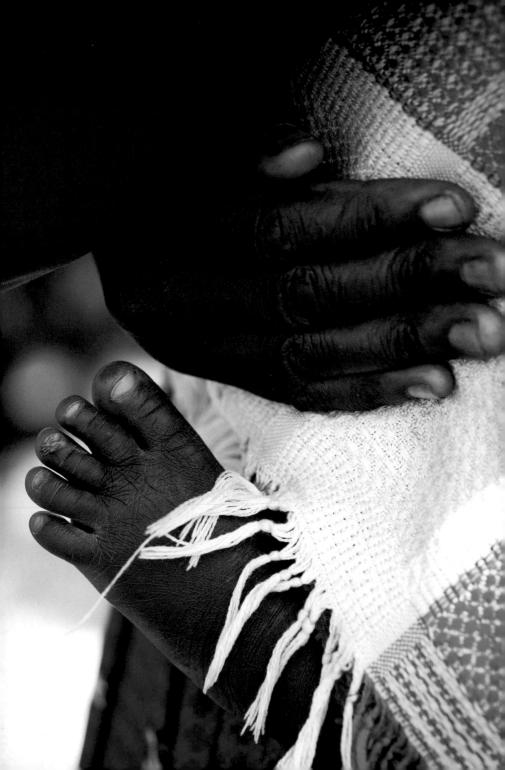

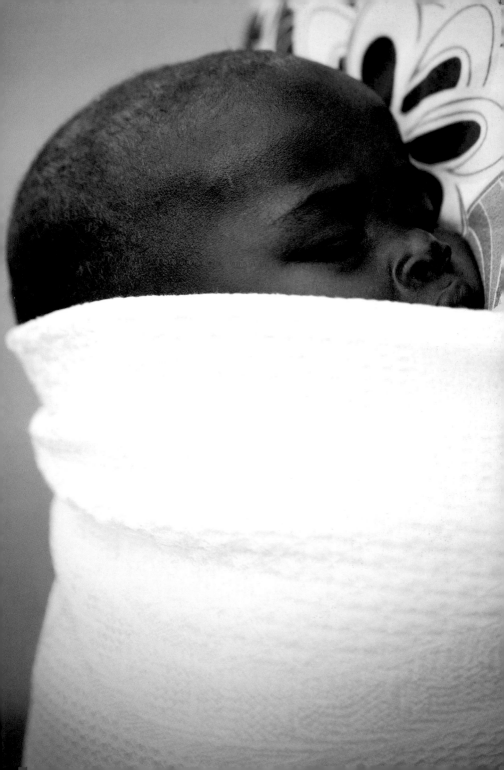

The rebels had taken control of the remote clinic and were using it to nurse their sick and wounded. Aided by a traditional midwife Lucy waited for the moment when her child would be born. She gritted her teeth and grasped the bed-sheet into her clenched fists as she felt her hips being pulled apart and her abdomen contracting. She was still just 15 years old and she felt that the pain was more than her tiny body could handle. She was terrified and she thought that she was going to die.

An Unwanted Child

Lucy had been in labour for two days and she was having a breech birth; the baby was facing the wrong direction and its feet were coming out first. Even if she had been surrounded by the best physicians in a well-equipped hospital, the complications were enough to endanger both mother and child. But here in the middle of nowhere, without access to adequate medicine or knowledge, Lucy could only push and pray for the best. She battled and struggled with all of her strength until finally Lucy gave birth to a healthy baby girl. But when she looked into the innocent face of her child, a seed was planted and Lucy began to hate her daughter.

Lucy had not yearned to cradle her child or to embrace her for the first time. She never wondered at the miracle of life, instead she saw the evidence of her misery, an ever-present reminder of her abuse. This child chained her to the horrible nightmare that she was living and now she could never escape. Lucy wondered what a broken, wounded, traumatised 15-year-old girl could give to this child. What prospect? What opportunity? But as she held her baby closer, heard her soft breathing and saw her big eyes blink in the bright light of day, Lucy's heart broke, not for herself, but for her daughter. She embraced her and whispered her name gently into her ear. Lucy called her Hope.

In the years that followed, Lucy had to learn to fend for herself, without relying on anybody to protect her or her child. George Komakech quickly grew tired of her, and he brought in many new wives - 23 other girls who, like Lucy, were stolen from their homes and forced into a life of bondage and abuse. She learned how to assemble and fire a gun and she carried it with her everywhere she went. If they came across the Ugandan army she was expected to fight her way out of trouble, with her baby strapped to her back. Each morning, she had to wake up early to search for water and firewood with her co-wives. Lucy was constantly on the alert, expecting that at any moment she might suddenly find herself in the middle of a fierce gun battle. She was always prepared to pick up her belongings and evade the crossfire with her daughter.

Carrying her tent, her provisions and baby Hope on her back, Lucy often walked many miles from one camp to the next. She endured endless uncertainty. Her life's only purpose was to survive each day so that she could keep her daughter alive. She had no other ambition, but to escape from captivity and return to her family, but she had no idea how she could do this. When she was 17 she had another child; a boy whom she called Daniel Ogen Wot, which means, "Trust in God." But Daniel died when he was only nine months old.

One day George Komakech suddenly fell sick and was taken to a clinic in Sudan by one of his wives. A few weeks later she returned with the news that he was dead. Joseph Kony was afraid that the death of his right-hand-man would discourage the troops, so he ordered Lucy and the other wives not to tell anyone. The actual details of her husband's death were kept a secret from Lucy and it was many years before she discovered the truth. After George Komakech died, Lucy and his other wives began to fear that other men would try to take advantage of their vulnerability. George Komakech was a feared and respected commander, and while he was alive, he provided them with some degree of protection. Now that they were on their own, any of the other commanders could harm them or claim them as their own. Some of the wives got together and began to plot an escape.

Escape

The field in which the women grew their vegetables was an hour's walk from the camp, and Lucy and the other wives made this journey everyday. One morning they gathered the tools they needed to dig in the field and walked towards the field but they never came back. For the next three months Lucy and the four other women carried their children and fled back to their homes. At night they hid in the bushes and the long grass. As they travelled, they watched over their shoulders to see if they were being followed. They managed to evade capture by Joseph Kony's soldiers. On one occasion, they encountered a local chief, who was an ally of Joseph Kony. He apprehended the women and intended to return them to their captivity. The women understood their fate - humiliation and a vicious death. Together they overpowered the chief and killed him. They knew now, that if they didn't make it home, they would certainly die.

Finally, Lucy and Hope arrived in Gulu. During her time in captivity her father had died, but her mother was still alive and Lucy was welcomed home with a loving embrace and tears of joy. As soon as she arrived, her mother encouraged her to register with an organisation that was helping to rehabilitate people who were returning from captivity. While she was there Lucy was given a medical check up and she learned that she had HIV. She was devastated, and when she returned home she didn't say a word to anybody. She feared that if her mother found out, she would be afraid and ashamed and she would evict Lucy from the house. She was terrified of her mother's rejection and she knew that she needed continued grace and love.

As she reflected on her life, Lucy began to believe that she had run out of options. Her life was characterised by disappointment and pain. She had hoped that, once she returned home, she might be able to start over and to make the most of whatever new possibilities might arise. But soon she became ill and she couldn't get up from her bed. She became weak and, slowly, she began to fade, to disappear into nothingness. Lucy knew that she was going to die and she embraced the lie that this was what she deserved. Death would bring an end to her misery and every poisonous memory of her life would die with her. Yes, this death, to be finished and forgotten, was better than to breathe and to eat and to perpetuate this meaningless and tragic existence. She fed on the lies and hatred of herself and of her story; hatred of her late husband who raped her and infected her with HIV; hatred of her daughter who carried his blood in her veins. She reached for her pill bottle, emptied the entire contents into her mouth and swallowed them.

"Right now I can stand firm knowing that God is there for me. I let go of anything that weighs me down because I know that God looks after me."

- LUCY LAKER

Lucy woke up in the hospital a few hours later and she saw her mother sitting by her bedside. The old woman was heart-broken but relieved that Lucy had survived. Lucy opened up her heart and revealed her bitter secret. She told her mother everything - that she was sick and dying; that she had hidden the truth because she was afraid that her mother, the only person who loved Lucy, would reject her. Lucy's mother smiled lovingly at her and said that she would walk this journey with her and that Lucy should never feel alone again. She encouraged Lucy to take her medicine and to decide to live the best life that she could. This is how Lucy began her journey back to dignity.

Lucy was one of the first 50 ladies accepted into Living Hope and she immediately found herself surrounded by love. When the Living Hope Centre was inaugurated in Gulu town, Lucy danced with her new sisters and they sang a song of celebration at the top of their voices. She learned how to sew and make handbags, dolls, and clothes. For the first time in her life, Lucy earned a salary. Slowly, stability was restored to her routine and she began to re-establish herself in the knowledge of God's love for her. She excelled in her craft and became a skilled tailor. At Living Hope she was introduced to ideas that changed her perspective and allowed her to break free of the things that tied her to the past.

Hidden Pockets of Hope

One day, during morning devotions, a woman stood up and spoke about unwanted children. Like Lucy, many of the women at Living Hope returned from captivity with children they wished they had never had. They saw in these children the faces of their abusers and they hated each memory associated with them. When the woman spoke she said that every child was a gift from God - even the ones who were born in captivity. She said that God had created them in His image, and that they were not accidents. She said that God had dreams and desires for these children and for the mothers who brought them into the world. Lucy understood that her bitterness towards Hope was paralyzing her and keeping her from experiencing freedom from the weight of her past. She regretted, and at times despised her daughter, because she was the link that constantly chained her to her memories. But now Lucy was learning to realign her perspective and to view Hope as a gift.

As Lucy, with purpose and intent, changed her mind-set she began to experience freedom. She asked Hope to forgive her for scorning her and telling her that she was unwanted. She chose to readjust her habits and started to encourage and embrace her daughter. Lucy told Hope that she was precious and valuable. She learned that, as she chose to love, she found hidden pockets of hope that emerged from somewhere within her, and this hope gave her strength. Soon Lucy flourished and excelled. She became an example of an unthinkable transformation and, with purpose and vision, she began to live out every aspect of her life with dignity and grace.

When she graduated from Living Hope's discipleship program Lucy was hired as a full-time employee in the tailoring department. A few months later, the owner of a local business came to Living Hope and asked to hire five graduates. Lucy stood apart as one of the brightest and the best. She began her new career, confident in her abilities and secure in her value.

Lucy arrived at Living Hope as a broken, wounded and defeated woman. A few years later, she entered her new workplace as an example of excellence; a signpost that displays to her community, the healing power of God's grace through Jesus.

ROBINAH NAKKONDE
A LIGHT IN THE DARK

"God will use them in His work of rebuilding, use them as foundations and pillars, use them as tools and instruments, use them to oversee his work. They'll be a workforce to be proud of, working as one, their heads held high, striding through swamps and mud, courageous and vigorous because God is with them..." - Zechariah 10:3

A gentle breeze stirred the old avocado tree and the leaves danced in the golden glow of the late afternoon sun. The fruit hung from thin, delicate branches, which swayed as the wind swept through Jolly's garden. One ripe avocado fell to the ground at a woman's feet. She reached out, picked it up, and put it into her handbag and continued to sing. A small crowd of 20 women lifted their voices together in a hymn of praise. Their eyes were closed, and their bodies moved gently to the rhythm as their lips softly shaped the words, as if it were a lullaby:

Tukutendereza, Yesu
Yesu Mwana gw'endiga;
Omusayi gwo gunnaazizza
Nkwebaza, Mulokozi*

A few feet away, just beyond the perimeter wall, where the road leads you to the busy shops and market stalls at Ntinda Corner, the city, bathed in sweat and dust, began to prepare itself for the oncoming darkness. Children returned home from school in small, staggered groups. They dodged the bicycles and boda bodas* that mounted the sidewalk and weaved between the groups of pedestrians and street-vendors. A large truck sped by and blared its horn. Another car had switched lanes to overtake a taxi that had stopped in the middle of the road to off-load passengers. The car and the truck swerved to avoid each other, and the drivers released their frustrations with a barrage of curses. Out there, the city, ruled by confusion and chaos, collided endlessly with itself. But here in Jolly's garden, these women knew that regardless of their circumstances, there was space for them. Here they could find peace from the turbulence that defined their lives. And so the rejects and the misfits gathered here to sing and to pray and to celebrate their deliverance.

Robinah sat and sang with the women in the shade of the old avocado tree. When the song was over she stood up and addressed the women with authority. They listened to her attentively, occasionally nodding in agreement, or voicing their approval. Then she began to moderate a conversation and the women talked openly about living with HIV. There was no judgment here, because all of them were equals. All of them had suffered from physical and emotional anguish. They all experienced some form of rejection or discrimination. But they had each found their way to Living Hope and were now amongst sisters who loved and understood them.

Ever since she was a little girl, Robinah wanted to be a teacher, and in a way, that is what she had become.

*(page 125) "Tukutendereza..." lyrics from a Luganda hymn of praise
*boda boda: a motorcycle taxi

After she discovered that she had HIV, she grew tired of the ignorant and misinformed views that were common amongst people in her neighbourhood. Once, she had believed an acquaintance who told her that ARV medications only quicken death, and so, when she was first diagnosed, she refused to take them. Other common attitudes caused people to shun those who were sick and so, many people hid themselves away, and died in solitude and shame. However, Robinah had a neighbour, who proved herself a true friend. She didn't allow Robinah to die, because she knew the truth from a lie. She intervened to save Robinah's life.

Robinah was forced to drop out of school in her second year of high school. Her father was a polygamous man who had eight wives and 35 children. Robinah's parents separated when she was young, so her grandmother and stepmothers raised her. When she dropped out of school, she felt that she didn't have any prospects. Robinah aimlessly wandered the streets of the small town where she lived and quickly grew idle and bored, so she decided to try her chances in the big city. She followed her eldest sister to Kampala and stayed with her there. Robinah hoped to find a job, or to help her sister start a business. But, she quickly learned that there weren't many opportunities for an 18 year-old girl who had not finished high school. Soon, she felt that her only hope was to find a man to marry.

Robinah's brother-in-law had a close friend who worked at the university, and he would often visit. When he met Robinah, he immediately liked her, and so his visits became more frequent as he began courting her. Even though he was 20 years older than Robinah, he was charming, and reasonably well off. He held a steady job and was intelligent. He was also handsome, and

Robinah liked the way that he treated her. All of her other suitors were young and unsettled and this irritated Robinah. The man had others wives and had fathered 12 children. Robinah knew this, but she was young and in love. When she was 19 years old Robinah was married to him and eventually, she had five children.

Robinah's husband came from a very large family. Ever since he was a young man he had worked hard and managed to acquire a few plots of land on a hill on the outskirts of Kampala. On one plot he built himself a house, then he portioned out a small piece and gave it to Robinah. He registered the title deed in Robinah's name and told her that if anything was to happen to him, Robinah could rest assured that nobody would take her land. Then he built a small room on Robinah's land and rented it out to earn some extra income. But her in-laws were suspicious and they grew spiteful. They often visited and would argue with Robinah's husband, saying that he was selling off their father's land. They regarded Robinah as an intruder who was stealing their property and they began to hate her.

Spiralling Out of Control

When they were first married, Robinah's husband treated her with kindness and he provided for all of her needs. It wasn't long however, before he began to secretly take on mistresses. Robinah suspected that this was the case; it was confirmed one day when she went to visit a sick friend who was in the hospital. Her husband had said that he had to be in another city for a seminar, but as Robinah walked by the maternity ward she saw him cradling a newborn baby in his arms. When he noticed Robinah, he tried to hide and make an escape, but she easily deduced that he was at the hospital to see a mistress who had given birth to his child.

Robinah suppressed her anger and suffered through the pain of her husband's betrayal silently and alone. Even though Robinah was hurt, she was afraid of how he would react if she confronted him. She depended on him and she didn't have anywhere else to go with her five children. When they were dating, he used to listen to Robinah and would ask for her opinion on certain matters. He used to treat her with respect. But once they were married his attitude changed. He was the one who paid the bills, and he felt that this entitled him to make every final decision, even the ones that concerned Robinah's well-being. If she ever questioned him or complained about something, he would rise up against Robinah with a terrible fury. When the marriage was in trouble and Robinah returned home to her father, she was immediately sent back to her husband. Wherever she went, Robinah felt that she didn't have a voice, so she decided that her only choice was to put up with his philandering and say nothing of it.

When her husband fell gravely ill one day, Robinah took him to the hospital. As she waited for the results of his medical examinations Robinah walked up and down the halls and noticed that some nurses were conducting HIV tests. One of the nurses asked Robinah if she knew her HIV status. Robinah laughed nervously, and said that she had never been tested, but that she was confident that she wasn't sick. Still, out of curiosity, and a certain sense of responsibility, Robinah agreed to be tested, but she wasn't worried. She sat down and playfully chatted with the nurses while they tied a tourniquet around her arm. Then they inserted a needle and extracted a vial of blood.

"Robinah suppressed her anger and suffered through the pain of her husband's betrayal silently and alone."

They wrote her name on the container and told her to come back in a week to collect the results.

Her husband died a few days later. He had not shown any symptoms that indicated that he had HIV. The doctors told Robinah that her husband died from tuberculosis. When Robinah went to collect the results of her test, she was still confident that the results would come out negative. To her great horror, Robinah found out that she had HIV. She staggered back home in an agitated, crazed confusion. Robinah tried to make sense of the news and finally convinced herself that the test must have resulted in some error. She returned to the hospital and was tested again. The results came back the same. Again, Robinah embraced denial. After a third test had confirmed her status, Robinah allowed herself to lament her situation. She returned to her house, shuttered herself inside and wept bitterly. Robinah was certain that she was going to die and she was not ready for it. When she told a few friends, they all advised her not to tell anybody. They said that if people were to find out, they would disassociate themselves from Robinah and her children. She felt completely alone.

A few days later, Robinah saw one of her in-laws sitting under a tree outside the house. The woman looked as if she was waiting for someone, and a few moments later another relative arrived. Robinah made nothing of it and continued with her chores. Later that day, Robinah left the house and walked to her neighbour's house, because she needed to buy some charcoal from him. She exchanged greetings with the man, and he asked if Robinah's visitors had arrived. Robinah was confused and gave the man a quizzical look. She told him that she wasn't expecting any visitors. The neighbour said that many of Robinah's in-laws had stopped by to see if she was around and he assumed that some family gathering had been arranged.

Robinah was puzzled and quickly became concerned. She rushed back home and when she got there, a crowd of about 20 of her husband's relatives were sitting on her porch dividing her late husband's property amongst themselves. Some people had entered the home and were removing her tables and chairs. In her absence a small truck had arrived and was being loaded with the children's beds. They were fighting amongst themselves and took no notice of Robinah who stood helplessly in front of her home while her relatives emptied it of every valuable thing.

Finally, Robinah shouted at the intruders and asked them who had given them permission to enter her house and take away her things. They looked arrogantly at Robinah as she trembled with fury. Someone responded, saying that they didn't need anybody's permission to claim the dead man's property. In fact, the intruder continued, everything that once belonged to Robinah's husband was now the rightful property of his brothers and sisters. As a widow, Robinah realised that she had no legal rights, and she could make no argument against them. She collapsed into a chair and watched her relatives fight for the small things that were still unclaimed.

On the porch a few women squabbled over a pair of bed sheets. Behind them a man reached up and pulled the curtains from the window, stuffed them under his armpit and casually walked away. Within an hour the relatives had stripped the entire house bare. They took every single plate, cup and saucepan. Even her baby's blanket was stolen. If Robinah had not hidden a few family photographs, the relatives would have left nothing by which the children could remember their father. She tried to salvage a few small things, but when the family discovered this, they pried the objects from her fingers. When they were done looting, they looked at Robinah and said to her, "Why are you still here? This is no longer your house. Get out." Robinah gave up. She turned around, and walked away.

Robinah moved next door into the small room that she had built on the land that her husband had given her. Her relatives couldn't touch her here, and, try as they might, they couldn't steal Robinah's land. Still, she had to endure the goading glances of her relatives. She watched from her bedroom window as they doled out the last remaining scraps of her former life. Often she wished to be far away from the people who had stolen everything from her. Instead, she was forced to look at them every day as they sauntered proudly in and out of her old house. With each passing day her resentment grew towards them, but there was nothing she could do about it.

Despondent

Shortly after losing her husband and her home, Robinah's only daughter, Diana, became suddenly sick. Robinah rushed her to the hospital, where the doctors suspected that Diana had swallowed something poisonous. Diana was only nine years old when she died and Robinah was tormented with grief. Within the space of a few months, her life had become an unbearable tragedy. Robinah knew that she needed to be strong for her boys, but she feared for their future. Every day she thought of death. She became discouraged and gave up any hope that she might live for more than a year. She often found herself lost, staring blankly into space, while she imagined her burial. She thought of her four young boys standing around her coffin, mourning her death. She pictured her eldest son dropping out of school, knocking on the door of the cruel people who had chased them out of their home, and begging for a piece of bread to feed his younger brothers. She lost the motivation to take care of herself and slowly Robinah disappeared into herself. Each day she removed a piece of herself - an aspiration, a dream, a desire - and discarded it. It was as if she was trying to become invisible, so that when death came for her, she would have already vanished, disappeared into nothingness. Though her body remained strong, Robinah's spirit was slowly being hollowed out by a gravity she could not overcome. She submitted to the idea of her impending death.

Despite all of this, Robinah managed to carry on her daily routine. Each day, she walked to the school cafeteria where she worked, and stood under the scorching sun. By the flames of a fire she had made, Robinah fried mandazi* and sold them to the school children during their morning break. As she saw the little boys and girls, with their big smiles and expectant eyes, line up to buy the snacks that she had made, Robinah thought of her own children and gathered the strength to carry on, one day at a time.

While her husband was still alive, Robinah had bought a storage tank in which she saved rain water, which she sold to people in her community. With this money she was able to send her boys to school and to buy them food.

*Mandazi - a local doughnut

I remember the first prayer that I prayed after my husband died. I said, "God, keep me alive; help me see my children grow." And He did.

- ROBINAH NAKKONDE

Robinah knew that with motivation and determination, she could do well for herself, but the knowledge of her fast-approaching death paralysed her. She didn't allow herself to dream or invest herself in the future. She thought that if she accumulated anything, her relatives and neighbours would rob her children once she was dead, so Robinah gave up trying.

While collecting water one day, Robinah felt an intense heat spread across her arm. Blood rushed to her head and she felt dizzy. It felt as if someone were pouring boiling water onto her skin. The pain was unbearable and the heat of the day was making it worse. Robinah checked her body and noticed that a rash had suddenly developed and was spreading from her arm towards her chest. She rushed home, locked herself in the room and closed the curtains around her. Robinah didn't want anybody to see her in her misery, and she lay in bed for four days, slowly wasting away. She had heard that HIV caused many people to suffer from strange and sudden rashes, and she wondered if the end was near.

Not Forgotten

Eventually a friend and neighbour, Mama Kabengano, knocked on Robinah's door. At first Robinah ignored her, but Mama Kabengano would not give up. She beat her fist on the windows and called out Robinah's name until Robinah relented and let her in. Robinah had not eaten for days. The fear and the pain kept her from sleeping, and Mama Kabengano noticed that Robinah had disintegrated into despair. When Mama Kabengano told Robinah that she was there as a friend to take her to the hospital, Robinah simply refused. She didn't want anybody to see her in this condition.

Mama Kabengano called a taxi and dragged her friend out of bed and took her to the hospital anyway. Robinah was diagnosed with Herpes Zoster, which was the cause of the painful skin rash and an indication that Robinah's immune system was failing.

A few friends rallied together and raised enough money to pay for Robinah's treatment, and within a few weeks she was much better. She began taking ARVs and, with the encouragement of the friends who had kept her alive, Robinah regained some hope. Her true friends had emerged when she was in her darkest moment and they had shown her grace.

Suddenly, Robinah no longer felt isolated. Instead, she felt loved and this changed her perspective. Robinah's friends had demonstrated that she was important and she found courage. Immediately, Robinah understood that she had allowed herself to be defeated because she was afraid, ashamed and misinformed. She decided to share her experiences with others because she wanted to help carry them to a place of healing, like her friends had carried her. Robinah grew angry at the lies that people had told her about AIDS, and she decided to speak the truth. She understood, better than anybody else, that lies led to pain, isolation and death, but truth brings new hope and the chance to be reborn. Ignorance and fear were killing hundreds of people in Robinah's community, and she set out to change that.

First, Robinah began to educate herself about the disease. She volunteered at Mildmay, a leading Christian charity that is combating the spread of HIV/AIDS in Uganda. Here she was trained to be a community outreach volunteer. She read books, she met with experts, she went to seminars and she talked with other women who had the virus. Soon, she realised that it was important for her to disclose her status. If she continued to hide the fact that she was an HIV+ widow, her secrecy could be misconstrued for shame, or ignorance. By going public, Robinah recognised that she could help others who were suffering just like she had. It wasn't an easy decision. She thought of her boys, and she knew that, at first, they would be teased at school. Some ignorant people might think that the children were HIV+ simply because Robinah had the virus, and she was afraid of the rejection they might face. In the end, Robinah understood that, by embracing truth, she could change the misinformed beliefs and harmful attitudes that brought so much pain to her community. And so, Robinah found the courage to speak up.

Shining Her Light

She began to listen for the neighbourhood gossip. If she heard of a woman who had locked herself away because she was dying from AIDS, Robinah would gather her courage and go to that woman in her home. Often, the door was slammed in her face, and although it was awkward, Robinah didn't become discouraged. She shared her testimony, but still, some people didn't believe her. They thought she looked too healthy to be suffering from HIV. This disbelief gave Robinah the opportunity to address the many common misconceptions about the virus. There were skeptics who chased her away, but many of those who allowed Robinah into their homes survived and enjoyed an improved life.

When a friend told Robinah about Living Hope, she initially didn't give it much thought. A few days later, she was collecting her ARVs when she met another friend who encouraged Robinah to visit the Living Hope Centre in Kampala. She agreed, mostly because she was now curious to find out what all the talk was about. When Robinah first arrived she instantly recognised a community, a sisterhood of women, who were motivated, focused and determined to improve their neighbourhoods. All of the women, just like Robinah, had a powerful testimony to share. They had all experienced terrible hardship, and they were all on their road to recovery. She fit in, and she understood that she could learn and develop her natural skills as a leader.

As she attended business-training classes, Robinah acquired the simple knowledge that she had missed when she had been forced to drop out of school. She learned how to develop a simple business plan, and how to manage her time and money. As she applied these lessons, she watched her business grow, and was able to support her family. At Living Hope, Robinah made friends. She learned to forgive the people who had stolen everything from her. Now, some of them even drop by occasionally to share a cup of tea in the new house that Robinah built on her small plot of land. Through discipleship and regular fellowship with the women and the staff at Living Hope, Robinah strengthened her Christian faith and she has developed into a strong leader.

Today, Robinah is a woman of great influence. She no longer fears rejection or discrimination. Instead the people in her community come to her for advice on how to manage the problems that they face. They call her "Mama," and Robinah greets them with a comforting and motherly embrace. She smiles often and she speaks the truth. Robinah does not compromise and she does not give up. She has been empowered. She is an example of true transformation. Robinah works tirelessly to rescue vulnerable women in her neighbourhood - those who are lonely, desperate, dying or ashamed. She leads them to a place of restoration and this is her passion.

JENNIFER AMONY
FINDING FORGIVENESS

"Can a mother forget the infant at her breast, walk away from the baby she bore? But even if mothers forget, I'd never forget you — never. Look, I've written your names on the backs of my hands."
- Isaiah 49:16

Jennifer knocked on her mother's door and called out to her again. Inside the tiny hut, her mother fidgeted and continued to ignore her daughter. A small crowd gathered, as neighbours, and people who were passing by, stopped to watch what was happening. Life in the IDP camp* was crowded and indiscreet. Here, it was impossible to keep secrets and everybody knew the gossip. Jennifer was a "returnee", one of the people who had escaped from a life amongst Joseph Kony and his LRA rebels. She was not welcome here. Jennifer felt the gaze of the crowd burning into the back of her head as she beat her palm against the door and pleaded with her mother inside. She blushed, and picking a handkerchief from her pocket, she wiped the tears that were now streaming down her face. Somebody in the crowd spoke softly, and though Jennifer couldn't make out what was said, she heard the word "returnee," and Jennifer knew that she had been marked out for shame.

*IDP: Internally Displaced People's Camp; refugee settlements established by the government to protect people in northern Uganda from the LRA.

The last time she was here, the same crowd had gathered and watched Jennifer's mother humiliate and disown Jennifer. "I don't want to see you again," her mother said, "forget that you were ever my daughter." Then she slammed the door and left Jennifer standing in silence. Jennifer tried to hide her face from the onlookers, but she was mercilessly exposed. She stood there voiceless and dejected and so she cried inconsolably. A sudden surge of hatred and bitterness erupted in Jennifer's heart. She felt crushed, forsaken and angry. Still, Jennifer had gathered all her courage and she returned again. "Maybe my mother will show me mercy today," she thought. Jennifer didn't want her mother's money; she wasn't looking for a place to stay, or for someone to look after her baby. Jennifer only wanted to tell her mother what she had learned about forgiveness. She wanted to show her mother that she loved her.

Living in Fear

The first time Jennifer was abducted, she was sweeping away the dry leaves that were scattered in front of her mother's hut. It was a Sunday morning and her mother had left early to go and dig in her field. She left Jennifer alone and told her to clean the homestead and wait for her to return. Jennifer washed the dirty clothes and laid them out to dry on the roof of the hut. Then she took a small broom, which was made from a single bundle of thick stalks of grass, which was tied together with a small piece of string. As Jennifer swept, a cloud of red dust lifted in front of her and the wind began to carry it away. She looked up and saw a group of men emerge from the dusty haze. They were LRA rebels and were walking straight towards her. Jennifer was only 12, and she thought that some of the men looked her own age. She froze on the spot, too scared to move. In the middle of the soldiers, Jennifer saw a group of nine frightened children, friends from her neighbourhood, who were tied to each other with a rope fastened tightly around the waist.

A few of the youngest soldiers, boys the same age as Jennifer, encircled Jennifer and told her not to be afraid. They said that they too had been abducted not too long ago. "Being a soldier isn't so bad," one little boy said, "I have a gun, and people fear me. If someone annoys me I can just shoot him." The other children smiled and laughed in agreement. Jennifer felt her throat grow tight and her heart pound violently against her chest. One boy told Jennifer to pick up a jerry can that was full of water and to carry it on her head. Then, with their guns, they pointed toward the tall grass, where they disappeared together.

After walking for four hours, the group arrived where their commander was waiting. Jennifer had a pulsating headache, her feet were swollen and her knees were throbbing from exhaustion. She felt ready to collapse. The commander took one look at Jennifer, and realising that she was too young and too weak to continue on the journey, he ordered one of the child soldiers to release her. "Don't worry," he said, "I know where you live. I will send my boys to find you again. Run home now, but remember this: I am coming back for you."

Jennifer ran as fast as she could. She could hear her heart pounding, and her lungs expanded until it felt like her chest might explode. Sweat poured down from her forehead, and streamed down her nose, before spilling in giant drops onto the dirt around her.

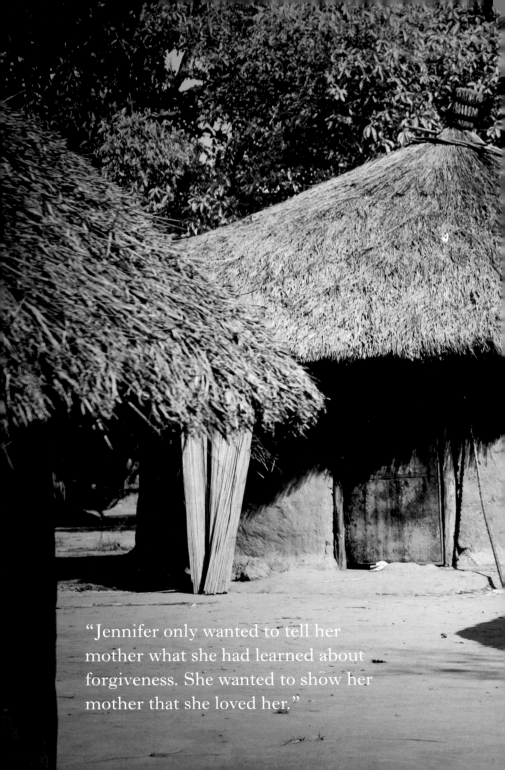

"Jennifer only wanted to tell her mother what she had learned about forgiveness. She wanted to show her mother that she loved her."

IDP camp in northern Uganda

Her mouth became dry and she was thirsty, but Jennifer kept running. She set her sights on home and she never looked back. Jennifer ran for what seemed an hour, but she quickly depleted her energy. Her legs became heavy, and her sides began to ache. Each step was a burdensome effort. Soon, she was no longer running, instead her feet clumsily dragged and tripped over each other in a laborious plod. But Jennifer's determination guided her home. When she finally arrived at her homestead, Jennifer's mother was waiting nervously by the door of her hut. She was ready to scold her daughter, but when she noticed Jennifer's condition she ran towards Jennifer and gathered her in a loving embrace.

That night Jennifer couldn't sleep. After several restless hours she got out of bed and went to her mother to repeat what the rebel commander had told her. The words escaped Jennifer's mouth like a gust of cold, dead wind, and they lingered in the damp, airless room, like a hidden, evil spirit, in search of a dark place to haunt, "I am coming back for you." Jennifer's mother tried to reassure her daughter. She said that in the morning she would take Jennifer to the town, where nothing could happen to her. The following day, Jennifer packed her few possessions and enrolled in a boarding school in Gulu. Jennifer was encouraged by the sight of people moving around town, and government soldiers patrolling the streets. Still, she could not escape the thought, that one day her tormentors would find her and take her away forever.

Jennifer adjusted well to life at boarding school. The routine of daily life provided her some welcome, and unfamiliar stability. Jennifer's parents had separated when she was a baby, and she had never met her father. After their separation, her mother met another man and formed a new family. There was no room for Jennifer in her mother's new life, so she was forced to move around from the house of one relative to another. Even though her mother seemed distant, Jennifer loved her and respected her. Jennifer's relatives noticed that she didn't have many people who she could rely on and so they treated her with compassion. Her mother's brother was especially kind, and Jennifer's grandmother had a particularly soft spot for little Jennifer. After she started boarding school, Jennifer's uncle invited her to stay with him and his family during school holidays. But there was still plenty of opportunity for Jennifer to be afraid.

Jennifer's uncle lived far from Gulu in a remote village, and because the rebels were a constant threat, the family would often hide in a thick forest during the night. Jennifer learned how to shape bundles of long grass into a tent, and to hide it from view. Like a soldier in a bunker, she tried to stay alert throughout the night. She made great efforts to develop the discipline to contain the urge to sneeze or cough. When startled by a caterpillar crawling up her leg in the middle of the night, she learned to maintain her composure. Jennifer didn't want anyone to hear her move the grass, or dry leaves of her tent as she rolled over on her dusty bed and she tried not to make even the slightest sound.

When they were in hiding, Jennifer didn't trust her cousins because she thought they were noisy and careless. She believed they would be easily found if the rebels came looking for children to abduct, so Jennifer hid alone, away from the group. She ran silently through the forest, and memorised the secret paths that she created. She took the endeavour seriously, never imagining for a moment, that any action in her meticulous routine was a waste of time or effort. Instead, she wondered if she was really doing enough to escape capture. Driven by fear, she was faithful to each gruelling task and always searched for new ways to perfect her hiding technique. If she heard a dog bark in the distance, or if a twig snapped as some animal passed near her tent, Jennifer's heart would stop and she would fear the worst. She imagined what life was like for her friends who were abducted with her not long ago. What kind of life were they living? Had they even managed to survive? Every night, as total darkness descended on her uncle's little village Jennifer would hear the words of the rebel commander resonating in her mind "I am coming for you." Even though she no longer stayed with her mother, Jennifer imagined the commander, watching her every move with a hidden, ever-present eye, and she was completely overcome with fear.

Living in Captivity

Jennifer was abducted for the second time when she was 14 years old. She was staying with her grandmother, and was not aware that the rebels were already in her neighbourhood by the time night fell. At about 10 p.m. Jennifer heard a knock on the door and the neighbours voice gently called out her name. When Jennifer opened the door she realised that it was a trap. Her neighbour had been captured and was forced to trick Jennifer into opening the door to the rebels. Jennifer's grandmother ran to Jennifer's protection and threw her arms around her granddaughter. She begged the rebels to have mercy on Jennifer, but they threatened to kill the old woman if she refused to be quiet. They seized Jennifer from her grandmother's grasp, and tying her to a group of 20 other children, they marched their victims into captivity.

Jennifer knew that there would be no release this time. Her heart sank, and she submitted to a desperate and bitter defeat. She felt cursed, subjected to forces beyond her control. For the past two years, Jennifer had feared this very moment. While she may have found brief glimmers of hope in a reassuring word from her grandmother, it now seemed obvious to Jennifer that her terrible fate had always been inescapable. Maybe her ancestors, or some evil spirit was delivering a cruel punishment for past sins, she thought. In the end it didn't really matter, the unavoidable truth is that Jennifer was now a pawn and a slave. The promise of a happy life was the first casualty In her battle to survive life in the bush

The rebels forced their captives to walk for many hours in the darkness of night. Finally, they stopped to rest until the morning. After sunrise, the children were made to stand in a line and they were examined in the light of the early morning sun. Some of the captured children were too small to be of any use. In the bush they would only get in the way, and somebody would have to take care of them, and so these children were the first to be released. There were a few who were sick and too weak to carry on walking and they were left behind. Finally, a few girls said that they were pregnant, and because the rebels thought it would bring them bad luck to harm them further, these girls were allowed to return home. Jennifer was one of the six girls who were forced to carry on the journey to the rebel's main camp.

When they finally arrived, Jennifer was taken to bathe and her captors forbade her from touching anybody or speaking until she had been "cleansed." The commanders considered themselves holy people, and the girls were put through a humiliating ritual in order to make them clean and fit to be a rebel wife. Then, a group of commanders lined up in front of the girls, who had been stripped naked, and they inspected them so that they could choose which one they wanted to marry. A young commander chose Jennifer. His name was Michael Okot and he was ten years older than her. At first, Jennifer hated Michael because he raped her often. But, she observed women in the camp and noticed that those whose husbands treated them well were stronger and more healthy than the other women. Their husbands brought them clothes which they had stolen while on village raids. They protected them from the fighting, and they didn't make them work too hard. Some girls were taken captive and used simply for sex. Others had to do all of the work that the commanders thought was beneath them. These girls looked frail, and battered. Their husband's took pleasure in humiliating them and making them feel useless.

Jennifer feared that if she continued to resent Michael she would end up like the dejected and defeated women she saw around camp every day. She quickly learned that in the bush there are no friends, and so she realised that if she submitted to Michael he might protect her. He confided in her that he was abducted as a boy, and had been forced to do things that tormented him. Michael now believed it was impossible to escape his own actions and so he was afraid to return home. He felt trapped and incapable of leading any other life than that of a fighting soldier. Jennifer felt a strange compassion for him, and she recognised in him, some of her own fears. Slowly she began to look at her husband differently. She saw him as a victim who had been coerced into this terrible life, and her heart broke for him. She noticed how he defended her from those who wanted to take advantage of her, and he treated her with a certain kindness. One day, Jennifer realised that she loved Michael. She did not expect it, and she could not explain it, but Jennifer felt connected to Michael in a profound way, and so she forgave him.

When she was 15 years old Jennifer became pregnant. She knew now, that she could never escape and return to a normal life. Even though she loved her husband, Jennifer had long since given up hope that she could make something good out of her life. The child that was now being formed in her womb would know nothing but violence, indecency and pain. Still, Jennifer thought of her baby as a gift, a small piece of happiness in this land of bitterness and misery.

A few months later Michael died in battle, before he got the chance to meet his son. Jennifer was given to another commander and was forced to be his maid. She grieved for her husband but the wives of her new commander didn't show her any pity. They treated her like a slave. They humiliated Jennifer and forced her to work, even when she was heavily pregnant. She suffered alone. When she gave birth to her son she called him Dickens Oweka, which means, "you have abandoned me." After Dickens was born Jennifer continued to serve the commander's wives. With baby Dickens strapped to her back, she had to wash their clothes, to cook their food, and to dig in their fields. Her life was now more miserable than she ever imagined was possible. Every day Jennifer hoped for an opportunity to escape, but she didn't have the courage to put any plan into action. She was tired of sweating and breaking her back, of investing every bit of her strength only to receive abuse in return. Jennifer longed for her grandmother's embrace and to watch her mother cradle little Dickens. She realised that she could not protect him from the commander's wives who often mistreated Dickens, and so Jennifer felt like a failure.

Jennifer remained in captivity for four years, until one day, when government soldiers ambushed the rebel camp. The rebels were caught off guard and their barracks were completely destroyed. Many of them managed to escape but they had nowhere to fall back to, and not enough provisions to sustain the entire group. The women and children quickly became a burden and so they were released and told to return to their homes. When Jennifer arrived back in Gulu she was taken, with the other women and children, to World Vision. Here, social workers tried to locate their families. With each passing day, Jennifer grew more anxious to find her mother. Finally, Jennifer grew impatient of waiting, and decided to search for her mother in the IDP camps.

Rejected

The camps were horrible places. When the war intensified the government had removed people from their remote villages and placed them in settlements closer to the towns. The army believed that they could better protect the population in this way, but the living conditions there were vile. Some 1.4 million people were forced out of their homes and into the congested camps, which soon became the prime target of rebel attacks. Many people who lived in the camps were massacred, or died from diseases which became prevalent in the tightly packed communities. People in the community despised returnees and looked at them as murderers.

Jennifer went door to door, searching for her mother. When she finally found her, she hoped to be greeted with a motherly embrace. Instead she was treated with shame. Jennifer's mother wanted nothing to do with her, and she wasn't interested in meeting Dickens. Jennifer pleaded with her mother to return to town with her, where she was renting a small room. Eventually her mother agreed, but she only stayed a few days before disappearing, without notice. During that time they rarely spoke and Jennifer's mother made it clear that she didn't want to be a part of Jennifer's life. Jennifer waited for her mother, but she never came back. Jennifer returned to the IDP camp, but her mother pretended that she wasn't home. Again, and again, Jennifer went back to her mother's hut, but her mother sat silently inside as Jennifer called out to her. Finally, one day Jennifer's mother emerged in a fury, and ordered Jennifer to get out of her life. She returned inside, and slammed the door behind her.

Anger and bitterness consumed Jennifer. She felt abandoned by society and betrayed by her own mother. She now felt unwanted, and unloved. Jennifer slipped into a deep depression and was overcome with loneliness. When she thought of her mother she was filled with rage and hatred. Jennifer now wished that she had died in captivity. It would be better, Jennifer thought, than to live in constant shame, knowing that she was so despised. Hatred took over her life. Poisonous thoughts and words surrounded her until Jennifer began to hate herself. She moved in with the first man who showed any interest in her. In time, Jennifer had given birth to two more boys. She hoped that he would love and comfort her, but he only took advantage of her. He told her that she was worthless because she was just a returnee. Jennifer believed him. After suffering for two years, Jennifer could no longer take the abuse. She packed her things and left with her boys to find another place to live.

"Forgive yourself for your past and don't let it hold your future. Otherwise your past won't let you see what the future has for you."

- JENNIFER AMONY

She survived by mending clothes, but was barely able to pay for rent and buy food.

When someone told Jennifer about Living Hope she didn't have to think twice. She was tired of struggling endlessly just to survive. Immediately, she registered and was accepted as one of the first women to benefit from the Living Hope discipleship program. At Living Hope, dedicated men and women from Gulu, people who spoke to Jennifer in her own language, welcomed her into a loving community. She learned how to read and write. She learned about Jesus' unconditional love for her. She learned about forgiveness through His grace, and she came to accept that God created her for great things. Circumstances, other people, and sometimes her own attitude had held her back. But at Living Hope Jennifer was introduced to ideas that changed her life.

A Parable of the Snake

Through trauma rehabilitation she began to process, and confront her history in a way that enabled her to open up new doors of hope and possibility. Most importantly for Jennifer, she learned how to forgive. Years of violation, abuse, abandonment and subjugation had scarred Jennifer and she was ruled by anger and bitterness. Throughout her life, other people had treated her like she was worthless, and they had denied her of any possibility of happiness and fulfilment. Jennifer blamed her ceaseless problems on those men and women who had stolen her innocence and her childhood. She blamed her mother for not trying to understand her, for disowning Jennifer and regarding her with shame and regret. She blamed society for despising her. All of these things had happened to Jennifer, but when she realised that she was not a slave to her circumstances, that she had the ability to rise above the evil that had been done to her, Jennifer understood that she could be free.

One day, Christine Lutara, the director of Living Hope in Gulu, illustrated to Jennifer the importance of forgiveness. She told Jennifer to imagine that she had been bitten by a poisonous snake and injected with a venom that was deadly. Jennifer would now have a serious choice to make. She could chase after the snake which had bitten her, and if she found it, she could kill it. But in doing this Jennifer would only enact her revenge, and the poison in her blood would soon kill her. Or, Jennifer could let the snake go, sit down, cut open a wound at the place where she had been bitten, and extract the poison now beginning to course through her veins. If she did this, though it may be painful, she would certainly live. Jennifer understood that she needed to forgive, for her own sake, all of the people who had poisoned her life. Many of them were already dead, and others were unwilling or incapable of changing their attitudes. Forgiveness was so important to Jennifer because in letting her snakes go, in extracting their poison, she was asserting power over the things that had controlled her for so long.

Encouraged by her new friends and mentors at Living Hope, Jennifer decided that she needed to repair her relationship with her mother. It had been several years since the two had spoken to each other, and when Jennifer approached her mother she feared another rejection. Yet again, her mother initially refused to see her, but through Jennifer's persistence and determination Jennifer's mother finally opened the door to her daughter. "I hope," Jennifer said to her mother, "that you will forgive me." She confessed her bitterness and feelings of hatred. Then Jennifer told her mother that she had already forgiven her. Sadly, Jennifer's mother remains distant, but through her persistent efforts Jennifer opened a door that once was shut. Her mother now welcomes Jennifer into her home and visits Jennifer's children regularly. While imperfect, the relationship is slowly being restored.

It was a painful process, and at times, Jennifer felt as if she was submitting to defeat. However, as she released herself from her past, Jennifer began to experience restoration in other areas of her life. By forgiving those who had damaged her so badly, Jennifer was able to concentrate on rebuilding her own life, and she began to heal.

Jennifer now understood that even though other people had rejected her, in the eyes of God, she was a gift, a special and beautiful creation. She began to feel valuable and to believe that she had potential. And so, Jennifer began to develop into the kind of person that carries with her an infectious joy. Now, you'll often find her at the Living Hope tailoring department, her locks of curly hair bouncing as she strides confidently across the room to supervise the cutting of fabric, or to help a woman new to Living Hope who is struggling to understand the sewing machine. She has become a leader at Living Hope and she trains women who have just entered the program. She has a radiant smile and a gentle demeanour and is always ready and eager to lead the ladies in a moment of spontaneous dance.

VIOLA LUTARA
IT TOOK A VILLAGE

"She is clothed with strength and dignity; She can laugh at the days to come. She speaks with wisdom, and faithful instruction is on her tongue."
- Proverbs 31:25-26 *

James Lutara's body was lowered into the wet, red earth. Even in death, it seemed there could never be a hole big enough to contain him. James had a giant personality, and now that he was gone, the space that he left behind was a devastating, overpowering emptiness. He died, as he had lived the rest of his life, optimistic, charming and ready to take on a new challenge. AIDS had reduced his powerful body to a delicate, brittle shell, but his spirit remained steadfast. At just 39, his life, still full of so much promise, came to a tragic end, and he left behind a wife and three young children.

Viola, stood beside his grave and watched as James' coffin was placed into the ground. She let out a cry that emerged from the deepest wells of sadness now buried in her heart. It came with a hollow longing; a lingering, unsatisfiable ache that pressed on her from every direction. She wanted to contain it, but Viola knew that she could not. Viola, now a single mother and a widow, was just 30 years old. "God," she prayed, "let me live until my children are old enough to care for themselves."

*(NIV)

Single Mother

Viola too, was raised by a single mother. She never met her father until she was in university. When her mother became pregnant, Viola's father already had a family of his own. Viola's mother was a strong, independent Acholi woman, and she threatened Viola's father, telling him that she would kill him if he ever came near Viola. As a girl, Viola learned to fear her mother, and to never question her.

Still she managed to learn a few things about her father that helped her to imagine what he was like. Her parents were from different tribes, he was a Muganda, from Kampala, in the south of Uganda, while her mother was an Acholi from a tiny northern town, called Palabek, near the border of South Sudan. Palabek was in the same district that the Lutaras were from. As a child, Viola knew, from a distance, the family into which she would eventually marry.

Viola's mother was a civil servant. At the time, the government ran businesses that produced and regulated the distribution of essential commodities such as salt and sugar. Throughout her career, Viola's mother managed several of these companies and she was stationed throughout the country. As a girl, Viola moved with her mother, and lived for periods, in various parts of Uganda. They made temporary homes in Hoima, in the west, Mbale in the east, Kitgum and Lira in the north, and Kampala in the south. Viola admired her mother's work and noticed how she went from being a clerical officer to a manager. Viola also wanted to be a manager, because she recognised the authority and influence that her mother wielded. In truth, the little girl didn't know what a manager was, but she was certain that she wanted to follow in her mother's footsteps.

When Viola entered high school, her mother sent her to a Catholic boarding school in Gulu. When she graduated Viola joined her mother in Kampala, and she enrolled in university. A few years later, while running errands one day with her mother in the city, Viola and her mother stopped at a clinic. Viola sat quietly on a chair in the doctors office while her mother and the doctor discussed some business matters. Viola observed the two for a moment, but soon lost interest in their conversation and became absorbed in her own thoughts. When the conversation was finished Viola and her mother returned to the car where Viola learned that the doctor she had just been visiting, was in fact the brother of Viola's father. Instantly, Viola knew that she wanted to meet her dad, and so it was arranged. When the two finally met, Viola's father had just suffered a stroke and was in a wheelchair. He apologised to Viola and expressed his deep regret that he had never been involved in Viola's life. Soon afterwards, he attended Viola's university graduation, and a few months later he died.

Not long before, in 1984, Viola met James Lutara at the wedding of one of her cousins. James had just returned from Germany where he had been living for ten years. He noticed Viola from across the room and was immediately attracted to her. As chance would have it, Viola's mother sent Viola to the house of the Lutara family with a gift. When she arrived, Viola found James sitting on the front porch. James knew that it was fate, and he became convinced that Viola was the woman he was meant to love.

James was a tall, loud and cheerful man. He was full of life. When in a crowd, it was impossible to miss James because of his deep voice, and his irrepressible laughter. He was a composer and a skilled musician, and he spent much of his time at a recording studio in Kampala. Although he could be shy at times, he was accessible and generous to a fault.

Viola and James soon began dating, and in 1985, when she was 21, Viola became pregnant. She gave birth to a daughter, Angela, but was still able to complete her degree, finally graduating in 1987. A year later, James and Viola were officially married and they joined the newlyweds fellowship at Watoto Church in Kampala. Soon, they welcomed a son, Lester, into the family. Viola landed a job in the civil service, and their family grew in love and in happiness.

James was a dreamer. He involved Viola in his aspirations and he treated her with love and respect. They went on dates together to the beach on the shores of Lake Victoria. Every day, James met Viola at her workplace, and they shared lunch. He told her crazy stories and made her laugh, and he was a wonderful father to Angela and Lester. He loved spending time with his children and the house was always full of laughter.

James came from a prominent family - his father had been a successful businessman and a Cabinet Minister. James believed he had the opportunities to develop his community and to help others, and he had ambitions to do so. He started a business, growing grain, peanuts and sesame which he sold to the World Food Program. He earned enough that he was able to get a loan from the bank and he started to build a house in Ntinda, a suburb to the north of Kampala.

Warning Signs

In 1992 James fell sick with a persistent cough that he couldn't shake. He contracted malaria several times within the space of a few months. Soon, Viola was taking James to the hospital once a month to treat some kind of flu or infection. His parents became concerned and suggested that the young couple get tested for HIV, but Viola found the suggestion outrageous. She had never been with another man.

Just to be safe, James and Viola went to their family doctor, who was a close personal friend, and they told him they wanted to be tested. The doctor dismissed them, perhaps a little embarrassed that a couple of their standing should come to him and ask for an HIV test. He said that there was no need for the Lutaras, a faithful, Christian couple, to be concerned about HIV. However, James soon developed a rash. He attributed this to an allergic response to the dusty working conditions at his workplace and he didn't think much of it.

Viola was now pregnant with their third child, Melissa, and was doing well until, at the beginning of 1993, she suddenly developed a lump on her neck. She didn't suspect it had anything to do with HIV because people commonly believed that HIV+ women could not survive a pregnancy. After Melissa was born, the lump on Viola's neck refused to go away, so her doctor decided to conduct some tests, which all came out inconclusive. Finally he agreed to do an HIV test, just to rule it out as a possibility. A few days before Christmas, the Lutara's left their blood samples at the clinic and went to Gulu where they celebrated the holidays.

Viola was certain that the results would prove that she didn't have the virus and so she had no fear. When the Lutaras returned home to Kampala, the doctor stopped in at their home to give them their results. When he arrived, he walked in the door with a certain air of sadness. Viola and James directed him to the living room and they all sat down together. "I have some bad news," the doctor said. Viola shuddered and asked, "Is it both?"

"Yes" the doctor said, as he solemnly nodded his head.

James and Viola sat in a numbed silence and considered their situation. Viola instantly knew that she was going to die, and for the first time in her life she felt hopeless. She wondered what her friends at church would think of her now. At this moment, Viola made a remarkable decision. She accepted her circumstances and chose to make decisions that would keep her alive. Viola didn't ask, "Why must I die?" Instead she asked herself, "What must I do to live?" She did not feel ashamed, even though she knew that some might shun her. Somewhere inside her spirit, Viola understood that shame lives in the secret places, hidden from the light of rational assessment, and beyond reach of the outstretched hand of redemption. She refused to concede to strangers the power to determine her value. Viola and James told their friends and family that they were HIV+ and in embracing the truth, they disarmed those in the public realm who might try to stigmatise them. Melissa, was just a few months old and they feared that she might be sick, but when she was tested, Melissa was free of the virus.

In 1994, just a few months after learning his status, James' health began to deteriorate. Rashes appeared all over his body and he had to stay at home more frequently. When Watoto Child Care Ministries was established to rescue orphans whose parents had died as a result of AIDS or war, James helped produce the first Watoto Children's Choir album. When he arrived at the recording studio, his body was wrapped in bandages that were concealed beneath his clothes.

As his condition worsened, James' business began to struggle. His trips to the farm to supervise the cleaning and packing of produce became more strenuous, and his body was taking a beating. Viola quit her job with the government and tried to help out. Things picked up for a while, but the problems became too much for James to deal with. His drivers began to steal from him, and on one trip one of his trucks overturned and James lost an entire shipment of sesame. He began to fall behind on the mortgage payments for the house in Kampala. As each day passed, and the levels of stress increased, James' body lost some vigour. The virus was eating away his resistance to common infections. ARVs were not yet available and James was forced to submit to a slow and steady decline, until he was eventually admitted to Lacor Hospital in Gulu, on June 6, 1994.

James was suffering from a severe throat infection. Every time he swallowed he experienced an agonising pain. He could no longer eat solid food, because his throat was lacerated with blisters and sores. Viola sat by James' bedside and would crack an egg into a glass of milk. She had to force James to drink the mixture because the pain was unbearable, and as she witnessed the agony her husband was going through, Viola wept bitterly. Unable to eat properly, James quickly lost weight and he began to show the hallmark symptoms of those who suffer from slim.*

*slim: local slang for AIDS.

Viola didn't ask, "Why must I die?" Instead she asked herself, "What must I do to live?"

Viola was still living in Kampala, and with the help of church members, family, and friends she was able to gather the money to make the long journey to Gulu to visit her husband regularly. A few friends took care of the children for long periods of time while Viola sat by her husband's bed and nursed him. James was in the hospital for 90 days, and even in the most difficult times, he tried to stay optimistic.

The doctors could only treat the opportunistic infections that were making him sick, however there was nothing they could do about his immune system.

Everybody knew that he was dying, still, James was an exemplary patient. He encouraged those who were around him. He never became bitter at his condition, instead his faith grew as he contemplated the end of his life. He fought, with all of his strength, to stay alive. Despite the endless pain he was in, James rarely complained. When his family or friends visited him in the hospital, they often left feeling uplifted, hopeful for a miraculous recovery. At the end of September, James was discharged from the hospital and returned home, but he was readmitted after only a month. He died a week later on November 5, 1994.

Viola sank into a deep sadness. She believed that her life too, would soon be over, and she wept for her children. Melissa was still just a baby, and Angela and Lester hadn't even finished primary school. What would they do once Viola was dead?

To make things worse, the family business was on the verge of failure, and Viola was unable to pay her mortgage, so she had to sell her house. Everything was falling apart. Viola's dreams and aspirations were now dead and buried with her husband. She lived each day just trying to survive the loneliness. The home, once filled with laughter and joy, was now choked by despair. When she looked to the future, Viola conceded that she could not survive by herself. She prayed for rescue and she left her fate in God's hands.

But, Viola was not alone. When she returned to Kampala, Vicky, a friend from her church cell group, visited Viola and discreetly gave her an envelope with enough money to pay Viola's rent, as well as the children's school fees. On hearing of James' death, Vicky had gathered a group of friends and collected enough money to support Viola as she adjusted to her new life. Viola's friends dropped by regularly, their arms full of groceries. Those simple, practical acts gave Viola the opportunity to rekindle her hope for the future. In making sacrifices in their daily routines and in their personal finances, Viola's friends showed her that she was valuable. The support she received from her family and friends continued, until Viola was able to manage for herself. Viola never went hungry. The children didn't miss a day of school. The family all went for regular medical check-ups and they were able to pay their bills. It took a small community of faithful, persistent people to keep Viola alive.

Generous Spirit

Viola learned to be honest with her friends, and she often had to swallow her pride in a moment of need. Sometimes she felt like a burden. "Why is it always me who needs to go begging for help?" she asked herself. She began to feel that she owed her friends a debt that she could never repay. But Viola soon realised that she had so much to offer. Viola became generous with her time, and she was always ready with a kind word of encouragement where one was needed. She soon realised the power of her testimony to demonstrate that people who are living with HIV, when given adequate support, can live and excel. She became an example of how a community can best respond to the suffering of those in their midst. Ordinary people, Christians who had an understanding of God's love for the hurting, had cared for Viola in an extraordinary way.

As Viola looked around she noticed that there were countless others who were suffering like her. These men and women, however, didn't have the support of their families. Their friends disappeared in their most desperate hours, and they were shunned. They suffered in isolation and shame because ignorant and selfish people cast them out and refused to associate with them. Some people were so rejected that when they died, their relatives refused to accept their bodies for burial. Viola's suffering was genuine, yet her experiences revealed that an early death was not inevitable, and that, with a little help, people affected by HIV can regain control of their lives. Viola understood that she could never repay her friends and family for all of their sacrifices, however she could invest herself in the lives of those who were not as fortunate as she had been.

Viola got a job working at the Uganda Revenue Authority and she was able to take care of her needs. Along with Maggie, a friend whose husband had died a few weeks after James, Viola started meeting once a week with other women who had recently been widowed. Viola invited the women to her home, and over tea and ginger cookies, they shared their experience of grief, depression and isolation. They prayed together and supported each other through their difficult moments. When Viola developed a rash on her arms and was embarrassed to go to work, her friends showed up at her door with a selection of long sleeve blouses, each a different colour and style, for her to choose from. Viola was encouraged, but the rash provided proof, for the first time, that Viola's immune system was getting weaker. She thought of how James had suffered so terribly, and she began to wonder how long she had to live. Viola wasn't ready to die, her children still needed her. She asked God to give her another ten years.

Only a few years after James' death, ARVs began to arrive in Uganda, but they were prohibitively expensive. The medicines cost more than Viola earned each month. Once again her friends rallied around to support her. Every month they scraped together whatever money they could spare and Viola was able to buy her medications. As soon as she began to take them, the rash went away, and Viola began to believe that she might live.

When Viola was just starting on ARVs, the medications were still in clinical trials and the side affects were severe. Each dose involved swallowing a fistful of pills, and every eight hours, Viola had to work up the strength to convince herself that the exhausting routine was worth the effort. Viola often felt nauseous. Sometimes she vomited the pills into the garbage and had to pick them out before trying to swallow them again. She couldn't skip a single dose and she had to maintain a strict diet. Viola carried a plastic bag in her purse, and while driving through the city, she often had to pull her car to the side of the road and wait for the nausea to pass.

"When the opportunity to be involved in Living Hope came up, it wasn't a matter of, *'let me think about it.'* It was a chance to give back. I keep telling the ladies that our stories are similar, we are just at different chapters. I tell them, 'you are also getting from point A to B because someone believed in you, and walked alongside you to keep you alive - to the point that you will then be empowered to hold someone else's hand and walk with them.'"

— VIOLA LUTARA

Sometimes she wanted to give up, but Viola knew that she was blessed to be surrounded by people who worked so hard to keep her alive. All around her, people were dying, simply because they couldn't afford the same ARVs that were keeping Viola alive. Over the next few years, the prices of ARVs came down and they became more accessible in Uganda. Viola became less dependent on her friends and family to survive, and she excelled in her workplace. Viola was able to send her children to university, and she adopted a little boy, Ashley, who was in desperate need of a loving mother.

When, In 2008, Watoto Church started Living Hope to restore dignity to vulnerable women, Viola stood out as the perfect person to help lead the new organisation. All of Viola's experiences prepared her for the unique role she plays in helping to restore vulnerable HIV+ women back to dignity. Armed with a unique understanding of the struggles that the women at Living Hope face, Viola is readily accepted as one of them. When Viola shares her story, the women understand that they too can live a life of purpose. Viola's background, the circumstances of her past, and how she lives her life make Viola accessible and exemplary. Viola's story is so powerful because it teaches us that our simple actions can actually make a meaningful difference. If it weren't for the "village" of people who unendingly believed in her value, Viola would not be alive. Because people understood her potential, and because they acted, Viola lives and improves her world, every day.

MARILYN SKINNER
AFTERWORD

God is doing something incredible in Africa. He is mobilizing a generation of wounded women, and raising them up to transform their communities. Where you and I might see oppression, God sees an opportunity to make evident His love for those who are in pain. Living Hope exists because we believe that God loves each and every woman, no matter what her circumstances. He wants to see all of us flourish as mothers, daughters and sisters. But, I've met far too many women who feel that they have nothing left to offer. Others simply have never been given the chance to fulfill their potential and realise their dreams.

The world is full of injustice, and it's easy to become overwhelmed. But I've seen how God can use simple, ordinary people like you and me, to bring His healing love to places in our world that need it the most. At Living Hope we have seen this happen. I'm in awe and humbled as people from all around the world, women and men have come alongside us. They have joined hearts and hands, given of their time, resources, and their love to ensure that their vulnerable sisters in Africa have the chance to stay alive and raise their own children. Their commitment to do what they can, with what they have, gives me the strength and courage to carry on. It enables Living Hope to restore dignity to some of Africa's most vulnerable women.

The journey has been a long and challenging one for many. I've cried with Nancy, a beautiful, innocent, 19 year-old Acholi girl who was abducted by the LRA when she was only nine. Nancy managed to escape from their cruel grasp, only to be abducted again. To teach Nancy a lesson, she was brutally mutilated. A child soldier sliced off Nancy's lips, nose and ears with a razor blade. Rejected by the community, Nancy was left defenseless and exposed. She lived in a prison of isolation, and hid herself away in the darkness of her hut, because she was ashamed of her appearance.

Living Hope held Nancy's hand as she underwent multiple surgeries to have her mutilated face repaired. And I wept with joy when Nancy looked into the mirror for the first time after receiving her new lips. Throwing her arms around me, Nancy wrapped me in a tight embrace and said, "I'm beautiful. I'm beautiful. Auntie, I'm beautiful." Nancy has learned that there is no one in this life so badly damaged that Jesus can't fix them. Because, when life gets broken, Jesus is an expert at putting it back together.

Today, Nancy makes peanut butter at the Living Hope Center in Gulu, and she sells sesame seeds in the local market. With her head held high and confident, and refusing to be defined by her past, Nancy's nightmares have been replaced with a dream that she can succeed.

Faithful sponsors from all over the world are regularly contributing in partnership with Living Hope, to improve the lives of thousands of women, just like those whose stories are written in these pages. My fellow Canadians have grown lavender and run marathons. Women in Australia have sponsored high teas and garage sales. Some have sold handmade jewellery. Others chose not to wear make-up for several weeks, in solidarity with African women whose faces had been mutilated. All of this was to facilitate reconstructive surgeries and put a smile back on another woman's face.

It's been exciting for me to see fellow Ugandans, moved with compassion for the plight of their own women. Young men in Gulu have helped our Living Hope Ladies produce sanitary towels so that girls can finish their education. In Northern Uganda, pads and tampons are a luxury, and huge numbers of girls drop out of school when they reach puberty because they have no access to this basic need. Girlfriends in the United Kingdom have donated thousands of panties to help keep girls in school.

Because of these partnerships, many women have been able to overcome and to prosper. Potential and creativity, that has for too long been locked up inside their shattered lives, has finally been unleashed. Hope has triumphed, courage has risen, and these women dared to dream again. Love, acceptance and affirmation have taught them how valuable they really are. Dignified help, demonstrated through practical empowerment, has given them the ability to provide for their own children, pay their own rent and buy their own medicine. Learning to read and write, so that they can help their children with their homework and manage a small business, has given them confidence to walk beside other sisters on their 'Return to Dignity.' Today, they stride through the streets of their neighborhoods, confident and happy. They aren't victims anymore. Now they live with dignity and purpose. They are infectious carriers of the most potent force in the world - the transformational love of Jesus Christ.

However, the Living Hope story isn't just for women in Africa, it's for women all around the world. You don't have to be a former child soldier, or an HIV+ woman in Uganda to feel abandoned or rejected. You may feel that way right where you are. God wants to restore every person back to dignity because He created every single one of us with purpose.

I believe God is doing something amazing with women everywhere. This is our day. He is gathering a group of everyday, ordinary women, from all walks of life, and He is calling us to rise up, and be what He has created us to be - beautiful light-bearers, filled with His glory, and conduits of hope to people who still feel hopeless. And that's the Living Hope story.

Living Hope is not just a program, it's a way of life. I have a dream that every woman in Africa will reach her full potential as she comes to the understanding that she's loved and that God created her beautiful, with a unique purpose and plan just for her. So that when the world looks at her, they will see that there is hope - living hope.

Marilyn

Living Hope's sustainable initiatives give women the opportunity to develop a skill and earn a regular income. At the Living Hope Centres in Gulu and Kampala women learn to make many items, such as jewellery, peanut butter, dolls and handbags.

If you've been moved by these stories of transformation through the love of Jesus, and you would like to partner with us to empower vulnerable women in Africa, please contact us at:

Watoto USA
13617 N Florida Ave
Tampa, FL 33613
866-492-8686
usa@watoto.com

WATOTO CHURCH AT WORK
WATOTO.COM